MAKING SENSE
IN THE
HUMANITIES

MAKING SENSE IN THE HUMANITIES

a student's guide
to writing and style

Margot Northey & Maurice R. Legris

Toronto
Oxford University Press

1990

Oxford University Press, 70 Wynford Drive, Don Mills, Ontario M3C 1J9

Toronto   Oxford   New York
Delhi   Bombay   Calcutta   Madras   Karachi   Petaling Jaya
Singapore   Hong Kong   Tokyo   Nairobi   Dar es Salaam
Cape Town   Melbourne   Auckland

and associated companies in
Berlin   Ibadan

Canadian Cataloguing in Publication Data

Northey, Margot, 1940–
    Making sense in the humanities

Includes index.
ISBN 0-19-540727-X

1. Humanities — Authorship. 2. Report
writing. 3. English language — Rhetoric.
4. English language — Style. I. Legris,
Maurice. II. Title.

LB2369.N67 1990   808'.0660013   C90-095759-X

OXFORD is a trademark of Oxford University Press
1 2 3 4 5 6 - 95 94 93 92 91 90
Printed in Canada by Webcom Ltd.

Contents

Acknowledgements

In preparing this expanded version of Margot Northey's *Making Sense: A Student's Guide to Writing and Style*, I received help from my research assistant, Kathryn Harvey and, in the early stages, from my colleague, David Jackel. To both of them my thanks. I owe a special debt of gratitude to the managing editor at Oxford University Press, Richard Teleky. His patience, tact, and friendly encouragement are here acknowledged with warmest gratitude.

Maurice Legris

Symbols for common errors

NOTE: If any of the following markings appear on one of your essays or reports, consult Chapter 8 or 9, or the Glossary, for help.

agr	agreement of subject and verb
amb	ambiguity
awk	awkwardness
cap	capitalization
cs	comma splice
D	diction
dang	dangling modifier (*or* dm)
frag	sentence fragment
gr	grammar or usage
mod	misplaced modifier
¶	new paragraph
//	parallelism
P	punctuation
quot	quotation marks
ref	pronoun reference
rep	repetition
RO	run-on sentence
sp	spelling
SS	sentence structure
sp inf	split infinitive
sub	subordination
T	tense
trans	transition
∩	transpose (change order of letters or words)
wdy	wordy
ww	wrong word

A note to the student

Contrary to many students' belief, good writing does not come naturally; even for the best writers it's mostly hard work, following the old formula of ten per cent inspiration and ninety per cent perspiration.

Writing in university or college is not fundamentally different from writing elsewhere. Yet each piece of writing has its own special purposes, and these are what determine its shape and tone. *Making Sense* will examine both the general precepts for effective writing and the special requirements of academic work (especially the essay and the report); it will also point out some of the most common errors in student composition and suggest how to avoid or correct them. Written mostly in the form of guidelines rather than strict rules — since few rules are inviolable — this book should help you escape the common pitfalls of student writing and develop confidence through an understanding of basic principles and a mastery of sound techniques.

This edition adds a new format for documentation in the humanities recommended by the Modern Language Association. (The traditional format preferred by many instructors is still included.) A new section on word-processors has also been added, along with advice on writing objective tests. The intent of the original remains: to give you a clear, concise, and readable guide that will help you do well on all your courses.

1
WRITING
and thinking

You are not likely to produce clear writing unless you have first done some clear thinking, and thinking can't be hurried. It follows that the most important step you can take is to leave yourself enough time to think.

Psychologists have shown that we don't always solve a difficult problem by "putting our mind to it"—by determined reasoning. Sometimes when we are stuck it's best to take a break, sleep on it, and let the subconscious or creative part of our brain take over for a while. Very often a period of relaxation will produce a new approach or solution. Just remember that leaving time for creative reflection isn't the same thing as sitting around listening to the stereo until inspiration strikes out of the blue.

INITIAL STRATEGIES

To write is to make choices. Practice makes the decisions easier to come by, but no matter how fluent you become, with each piece of writing you will still have to choose.

You can narrow the field of choice from the start if you realize that you are *not* writing for anybody, anywhere, for no particular reason. In university (or anywhere else), it's always sound strategy to ask yourself two basic questions: "What is the purpose of this piece of writing?" and "What is the reader like?" Your first reaction may be "Well, I'm writing for my teacher to satisfy a course requirement." But that's not specific enough. To be useful, your answers have to be precise.

Think about the purpose

Your purpose may be any one or two of several possibilities:
- to show that you understand certain terms or theories;
- to show that you can do independent research;
- to apply a specific theory to new material;
- to provide information;
- to show your knowledge of a topic or text;
- to show that you can think critically or creatively.

Certainly an assignment designed to see if you have read and understood specific material calls for a different approach from one that's meant to test your critical thinking or research skills. If you don't determine the exact purpose, you may find yourself working at cross purposes—and wasting a lot of time.

Think about the reader

Thinking about the reader does *not* mean playing up to the teacher. To convince a particular person that your own views are sound, you have to consider his or her way of thinking. If you are writing a paper on Israeli communes for a sociology professor, obviously your analysis will be different from what it would be if you were writing for an economics or history professor. You will have to make specific decisions about the terms you should explain, the background information you should supply, and the details you need to convince that particular reader. In the same way, if your reader supports the idea of a common market between Canada and the United States and you intend to propose higher tariffs, you will have to anticipate any arguments that may be raised, in order to answer them. If you don't know who will be reading your paper—your professor, your tutorial leader, or a marker—just imagine someone intelligent, knowledgeable, and interested, skeptical enough to question your ideas but flexible enough to adopt them if your evidence is convincing.

Think about the length

Before you start writing, you will also need to think about the length of your assignment in relation to the time you have available to spend on it. If both the topic and the length are prescribed, it should be fairly easy for you to assess the level of detail required and the amount of research you need to do. If only the length is prescribed, that restriction will help you decide how broad or how narrow a topic you should choose (see p. 9).

Think about the tone

In everyday writing to friends you probably take a casual tone, but academic writing is usually more formal. The exact degree of formality required will depend on the kind of assignment and instruction you have been given. In some cases—say, if your psychology or philosophy professor asks you to express yourself freely and personally in a journal—you may well be able to use an informal style. Essays and reports, however, require a more formal tone. What kind of style is too informal for most academic work? Here are the main signs:

Use of slang

Although the occasional slang word or phrase may be useful for special effect, frequent use of slang is not acceptable. The reason is that slang expressions are usually regional and short-lived: they may mean different things to different groups at different times. (Just think of how widely the meanings of *hot* and *cool* can vary, depending on the circumstances.)

Excessive use of first-person pronouns

Since a formal essay is not a personal outpouring, you want to keep it from becoming *I*-centred. It's certainly acceptable to use the occasional first-person pronoun, and your reader will obviously want to know your opinions—as long as they are backed by evidence. Still, you should avoid the *I think* or *in my view* approach when the fact or argument speaks for itself. If the choice, however, is between using *I* and creating a tangle of passive constructions, it's almost always better to choose *I*. (A hint: when you do use *I*, it will be less noticeable if you place it in the middle of the sentence rather than at the beginning.)

Frequent use of contractions

Generally speaking, contractions such as *can't* and *isn't* are not suitable for academic writing, although they may be fine for letters or other informal kinds of writing—for example, this handbook. The problem with trying to avoid excessive informality is that you may be tempted to go to the other extreme. If your writing sounds stiff or pompous, you may be using too many high-flown phrases, long words, or passive contructions (see Chapter 8).

2
WRITING
an essay

If you are one of the many students who dread writing an academic essay, you will find that following a few simple steps in planning and organizing will make the task easier—and the result better.

THE PLANNING STAGE

Some students claim they can write essays without any planning at all. On the rare occasions when they succeed, their writing is usually not as spontaneous as it seems: in fact, they have thought or talked a good deal about the subject in advance, and come to the task with some ready-made ideas. More often, trying to write a lengthy essay without planning just leads them to frustration. They get stuck in the middle and don't know how to finish, or suddenly realize that they are rambling off in all directions.

In contrast, most writers say that the planning, or pre-writing, stage is the most important part of the whole process. Certainly the evidence shows that poor planning usually leads to disorganized writing; in the majority of students' essays the single greatest improvement would not be better research or better grammar, but better organization.

This insistence on planning doesn't rule out exploratory writing (see p. 14). Many people find that the act of writing itself is the best way to generate ideas or overcome writer's block; the hard decisions about organization come after they've put something down on the page. Whether you organize before or after you begin to write, however, at some point you need to plan.

Reading primary material

Primary material is the direct evidence—usually books or articles—on which you will base your essay. Surprising as it may seem, the best way to begin working with this material is to give it a fast initial skim. Don't just start reading from cover to cover: first look at the table of contents, scan the index, and read the preface or introduction to get a sense of the author's purpose and plan. Getting an overview will allow you to focus your questions for a more purposeful and analytic second reading. Make no mistake: a superficial reading is *not* all you need. You still have to work through the material carefully a second time. But an initial skim followed by a focused second reading will give you a much more thorough understanding than one slow plod ever will.

A warning about secondary sources

Always be sure you have a firm grasp of the primary material before you turn to secondary sources (commentaries on or analyses of the primary source). Instructors in some subjects discourage secondary reading in introductory courses because they know the dangers of relying too heavily on it. If you turn to commentaries as a way around the difficulty of understanding the primary source, you may be overwhelmed by the weight of authority and produce a trite, second-hand essay. Your interpretation could even be downright wrong, since at this stage you may not know enough about a subject to be able to evaluate the commentary. Secondary sources are an important part of learning, and essential to many research papers, but they can never substitute for your own active reading of the primary material.

Analyse your subject: ask questions

Some instructors ask students to choose their own essay topics, and others simply suggest subject areas. In either case, since a subject area is bound to be too broad for an essay topic, you will have to analyse it in order to find a way of limiting it. The best way of analysing is to ask questions that will lead to useful answers.

How do you form that kind of question? Journalists approach their stories through a five-question formula: *who? what? where? when? why?* You could apply the same formula to aspects of your subject, and add *how?* For example, starting with the question *what?* and applying it to a work of literature, you might ask, "What contrasts of character can one find?''; ''What role do the minor characters play?''; ''What are the good or evil qualities of the characters?'' *How* and *why* questions are often the most productive, since they take you beyond information-gathering and force you to analyse and interpret. If you are considering the Canadian constitution, for example, you might ask, "How are the courts likely to be affected by the new constitution?"; "Why was education left to the provinces?"

Try the three-C approach

A more systematic scheme for analysing a subject is the three-C approach. It forces you to look at a subject from three different perspectives, asking basic questions about *components, change,* and *context*:

What are the components of the subject? In other words, how might it be broken down into smaller elements? This question forces you to take a close look at the subject and helps you avoid over-simplification. Suppose that your assignment is to discuss the policies of Mackenzie King. After asking yourself about components, you might decide that you can split the subject into (1) domestic policies and (2) foreign policies. Alternatively, you might divide it into (1) economic policies, (2) social policies, and (3) political policies. Then, since these components themselves are fairly broad, you might break them down further. Economic policies might be split into fiscal and monetary policies; political policies could be split into relations with the provinces and relations with other countries.

Similarly, if you are analysing the imagery in a work of literature, you could ask, "What are the different types?" (Think, for example, of similes, metaphors, and allusions.) Or you could ask, "What are the content groupings?" (for instance, animal images, solar images, or military images).

What features of the subject reflect change? For example, did Mackenzie King's policies in a certain area alter over a period of years? Did he express contradictory views in different documents? What caused changes in policy? What were the effects of these changes? For a sociological subject such as juvenile delinquency, you might ask, "Have there been changes in the rate of criminal offences committed?" or "Have there been changes in the nature or definition of delinquency?" Then ask, "What are the causes or effects of these changes?"

What is the context of this subject? Into what particular school of thought or tradition does it fit? What are the similarities and differences between this subject and related ones? For example, how do Mackenzie King's policies compare with those of other Liberal Prime Ministers? With Conservative policies? Turning to the subject of juvenile delinquency again, you might consider the nature or rate of delinquency in Canada as compared to that in other countries, or relate juvenile delinquency to problems in the adult population.

General as most of these questions are, you will find that they stimulate more specific questions—and thoughts—about the material, from which you can choose your topic and formulate a thesis. Remember that the ability to ask intelligent questions is one of the most important, though often underrated, skills that you can develop for any work, in university and outside.[1]

Analysing a prescribed topic

Even if the topic of your essay is supplied by your instructor, you still need to analyse it carefully. Try underlining key words to make sure that you don't neglect anything. Distinguish the main focus from subordinate concerns. A common error in dealing with prescribed topics is to emphasize one portion while giving short shrift to another. Give each part its proper due—and make sure that you actually do what the instructions tell you to do. To *discuss* is not the same as to *evaluate* or *trace*; to *compare* means to show differences as well as similarities. These verbs tell you how to approach the topic; don't confuse them.

Develop a hypothesis

Not all essays are arguments, nor do they all require a specific thesis. Yet most students find it helpful to think of an academic essay as a way of demonstrating or proving a point, since the argumentative form is the easiest to organize and the most likely to produce forceful writing. A hypothesis is nothing more than a working thesis—an intended line of argument which you are free to change at any stage of your planning. It works as a linchpin, holding together your information and ideas as you organize. It will help you to define your intentions, make your research more selective, and focus your essay.

At some point in the writing process you will probably want to make your hypothesis into an explicit thesis statement that can appear in your introduction. In any case, you should take the time to work out your thesis carefully. Use a complete sentence to express it, and above all make sure that it is *limited*, *unified*, and *exact*.[2]

Make it limited

A limited thesis is one that is narrow enough to be workable. Suppose, for example, that your general subject is the Social Credit party in Canada. Such a subject is much too broad to be handled properly in an essay of one or two thousand words: you must limit it in some way and create a line of argument for which you can supply adequate supporting evidence. Following the analytic questioning process, you might find that you want to restrict it by time: "The Social Credit party in the 1970s was indistinguishable in its monetary policies from the Conservative party." Or you might prefer to limit it by geography: "The development of the Social Credit party in British Columbia had less to do with its policies than with its political opportunities."

To take an example from literature, suppose that your general subject for a two-thousand-word essay is the work of Hugh MacLennan. You might want to limit it by discussing a prominent theme in one or two novels: "Although MacLennan exposes the dark side of religion in *Each Man's Son*, he also reveals a yearning for spiritual wholeness." Or you could focus on some aspect of characterization: "In *Each Man's Son* and *The Watch That Ends the Night*, MacLennan creates drama through his contrast of character types." Whatever the discipline or subject, make sure that your topic is restricted enough that you can explore it in depth.

Make it unified

To be unified, your thesis must have one controlling idea. Beware of the double-headed thesis: "In his term as President of the United States, Lyndon Johnson introduced many social programs, but the Vietnam War issue led to his downfall." What is the controlling idea here? The success of Johnson's social programs, or the reason for his downfall? The essay should focus on one or the other. It is possible to have two or more related ideas in a thesis, but only if one of them is clearly in control, with all the other ideas subordinated to it: "Despite criticism from various regions in Canada, the CBC is an instrument of national unity."

Make it exact

It's important, especially in a thesis, to avoid vague terms such as *interesting* and *significant*, as in "Helmut Schmidt was Germany's most interesting Chancellor." Does *interesting* mean *effective* or *daring* in his policies, or does it mean personally *charming*? Don't say simply "Sheila Watson's use of symbols is an important feature of her writing" when you can be more precise about the work you are discussing, the kind of symbols you've found there, and exactly what they do: "In *The Double Hook*, Sheila Watson adapts traditional symbols from Christian and Indian mythology to underscore the theme of spiritual death and regeneration." Remember to be as specific as possible in creating a thesis, in order to focus your essay. Don't just make an assertion—give the main reasons for it. Instead of saying simply "Many westerners are resentful of central Canada" and leaving it at that, add an explanation: ". . . because of historic grievances, such as tariffs and freight rates, and contemporary issues such as the energy policy and the new constitution." If these details make your thesis stylistically cumbersome, don't worry. A thesis is only a planning device, something to guide the organization of your ideas. The wording doesn't have to be the same in your final essay.

Research your topic

If your topic requires more facts or evidence than the primary material provides, or if you want to know other people's opinions on the subject, you will need to visit the library for research. Some students like to read around in the subject area before they decide on an essay topic; for them, the thesis comes after the exploration. You may find this approach useful for some essays, but generally it's better to narrow your scope and plan a tentative thesis before you turn to secondary sources—you'll save time and produce a more original essay.

Explore the library

The importance of getting to know your way around a library can't be stressed enough. You don't want to be so overwhelmed by its size and complexity that you either scrimp on required research or waste time and energy trying to find information. Remember that most academic libraries have orientation seminars specifically designed to show you where and how to find what you want—how to use a card catalogue, for example. Take advantage of these services. Librarians will be glad to show you the bibliographies, indices, and other reference books for your field of study. Once you are familiar with these basic sources you will be able to check systematically for available material.

Taking good notes

Finding your research material is one thing; taking notes that are dependable and easy to use is another. With time you will develop your own best method, but for a start you might try the index-card system. Record each new idea or piece of evidence on a separate card (see below); the number you need will obviously depend on the range and type of your research. When you've finished with your note-taking, you can then easily arrange the cards in the order in which you will use them.

ARNOLD J. TOYNBEE, A Study of History.
Abridgement of vols. I-IV by D.C. SOMERVELL
(New York and London: Oxford Univ. Press, 1946).

Says 20th century follows "typical pattern of
a time of troubles: a breakdown, a rally and
a second relapse" (p. 553).

Index Card

Whatever method you follow, remember that exact records are essential for proper footnotes:

1. For every entry check that the bibliographic details are complete, including the name of the author, title, place and date of publication, and page number, as well as the library call number. Nothing is more frustrating than using a piece of information in an essay only to find that you aren't sure where it came from. If you take several ideas from one source, it helps to put the main bibliographic details about the author and work on one card,

and then use a separate card for each particular idea or theory.
2. Check that quotations are copied precisely.
3. Include page numbers for every reference, even if you paraphrase or summarize the idea rather than copy it word for word.

A warning about plagiarism

Plagiarism is a form of stealing; as with other offences against the law, ignorance is no excuse. The way to avoid it is to give credit where credit is due. If you are using someone else's idea, acknowledge it, even if you have changed the wording or just summarized the main points. You may give credit either directly in the text ("As Toynbee says, . . .") or in a footnote. (For footnote style, see Chapter 11.) Don't be afraid that your work will seem weaker if you acknowledge the ideas of others. On the contrary, it will be all the more convincing: serious academic treatises are almost always built on the work of preceding scholars.

Where should you draw the line on acknowledgements? As a rule you don't need to give credit for anything that's common knowledge. You wouldn't footnote the well-known sayings of Jesus, for example, or lines from "O Canada," or the date of Confederation; however, you should acknowledge any clever turn of phrase that is neither well known nor your own. And always document any unfamiliar fact or claim — statistical or otherwise — or one that's open to question.

Creating an outline

Individual writers differ in their need for a formal plan. Some say that they never have an outline, and others maintain they can't write without one; most fall somewhere in between. Since organization is such a common problem, though, it's a good idea to know how to draw up an effective plan. Of course, the exact form it takes will depend on the pattern you use to develop your ideas — whether you are defining, classifying, or comparing, for example (see pp. 15-17).

If you have special problems with organizing material, your outline should be formal, in complete sentences. On the other hand, if your mind is naturally logical, you may find it's enough just to jot down a few words on a scrap of paper. For most students, an informal but well-organized outline in point form is the most useful model:

THESIS: When Trudeau first came to power, his style was seen as an enormous asset, but by the '80s the same style was increasingly seen as a liability.

    I. Trudeau's early style perceived in positive light
        A. Charismatic
            1. Public adulation: "Trudeaumania"
            2. Media awe
        B. Intellectual
        C. Tough
            1. Handling of journalists
            2. Handling of Quebec
        D. Anti-establishment
            1. Swinging lifestyle
            2. Disregard for government traditions
   II. Later reversal: Trudeau's image becomes negative
        A. Irritating
            1. Public opinion polls
            2. Media disenchantment
        B. Out of touch with economic reality
        C. Confrontationist
            1. With individual dissenters
            2. With Premiers
            3. With Opposition leaders
        D. Arrogant
            1. Extravagant lifestyle in time of recession
            2. Autocratic approach to governing

The guidelines for this kind of outline are simple:

Code your categories. Use different sets of markings to establish the relative importance of your entries. The example here moves from roman numerals to letters to arabic numbers, but you could use another system.

Categorize according to importance. Make sure that only items of equal value are put in equivalent categories. Give major points more weight than minor ones.

Check lines of connection. Make sure that each of the main categories is directly linked to the central thesis; then see that each subcategory is directly linked to the larger category that contains it. Checking these lines of connection is the best way of preventing essay muddle.

Be consistent. In arranging your points, be consistent. You may choose to move from the most important point to the least important, or vice versa, as long as you follow the same order every time.

Use parallel wording. Phrasing each entry in a similar way will make it easier to be consistent in your presentation.

One final word: be prepared to change your outline at any time in the writing process. An outline is not meant to put an iron clamp on your thinking, but to relieve anxiety about where you're heading. A careful outline prevents frustration and dead ends—that "I'm stuck, where can I go from here?" feeling. But since the very act of writing will usually generate new ideas, you should be ready to modify your original plan. Just remember that any new outline must have the consistency and clear connections required for a unified essay.

THE WRITING STAGE

Writing the first draft

Rather than labouring for excellence from scratch, most writers find it easier to write the first draft as quickly as possible and do extensive revisions later. However you begin, you can't expect the first draft to be the final copy. Skilled writers know that revising is a necessary part of the writing process, and that the care taken with revisions makes the difference between a mediocre essay and a good one.

You don't need to write all parts of the essay in the same order in which they are to appear in the final copy. In fact, many students find the introduction the hardest part to write. If you face the first blank page with a growing sense of paralysis, try leaving the introduction until later, and start with the first idea in your outline. If you feel so intimidated that you haven't even been able to draw up an outline, you might try John Trimble's approach and charge right ahead with **any kind of beginning**—even a simple **"My first thoughts on this subject are . . .".**[3] Instead of sharpening pencils or running out for a snack, try to get going. Don't worry about grammar or wording; scratch out pages or throw them away if you must. Remember, the object is to get your writing juices flowing.

Of course, you can't expect this kind of exploratory writing to resemble the first draft that follows an outline. You will probably need to do a great deal more changing and reorganizing, but at least you will have the relief of seeing words on a page to work with. Many experienced writers—and not only those with writer's block—find this the most productive way to proceed.

Developing your ideas: some common patterns

The way you develop your ideas will depend on your essay topic, and topics can vary enormously. Even so, most essays follow one or another of a handful of basic organizational patterns. Here's how to use each pattern effectively.

1. Defining

Sometimes a whole essay is an extended definition, explaining the meaning of a term that is complicated, controversial, or simply important to your field of study: for example, *nationalism* in political science, or *monetarism* in economics, or *existentialism* in philosophy. More often, perhaps, you may want to begin a detailed discussion of a topic by defining a key term, and then shift to a different organizational pattern. In either case, make your definition exact. It should be broad enough to include all the things that belong in the category and at the same time narrow enough to exclude things that don't belong. A good definition builds a kind of verbal fence around a word, herding together all the members of the class and cutting off all outsiders.

For any discussion of a term that goes beyond a bare definition, you should, of course, give concrete illustrations or examples; depending on the nature of your essay, these could vary in length from one or two sentences to several paragraphs or even pages. If you are defining monetarism, for instance, you would probably want to discuss at some length the theories of leading monetarists.

In an extended definition, it's also useful to point out the differences between the term and any other that is connected with it or often confused with it. For instance, if you are defining *pathos* you might want to distinguish it from *tragedy*; if you are defining *common law*, you might want to distinguish it from *statute law*.

2. Classifying

Classifying means dividing something into its separate parts according to a given principle of selection. The principle or criterion may vary; you could classify crops, for example, according to how they grow (above the ground or below the ground), how long they take to mature, or what climatic conditions they require; members of a given population might be classified according to age group, occupation, income, and so on. If you are organizing your essay by a system of classification, remember the following:

- All members of a class must be accounted for. If any are left over, you need to alter some categories or add more.
- Categories can be divided into subcategories. You should con-

sider using subcategories if there are significant differences within a category. If, for instance, you are classifying the work force according to occupation, you might want to create subcategories according to income level or sex.

- Any subcategory should contain at least two items.

3. Explaining a process

This kind of organization shows how something works or has worked, whether it be the weather cycle, the process of justice, or the stages in a political or military campaign. The important point to remember is to be systematic, to break down the process into a series of steps or stages. Although at times it will vary, most often your order will be chronological, in which case you should see that the sequence is accurate and easy to follow. Whatever the arrangement, you can generally make the process easier to follow if you start a new paragraph for each new stage.

4. Tracing causes or effects

A cause-or-effect analysis is really a particular kind of process discussion, in which certain events are shown to have led to or resulted from other events. Usually you are explaining *why* something happened. The main warning here is to avoid over-simplifying. If you are tracing causes, distinguish between a direct cause and a contributing cause, between what is a condition of something happening and what is merely a correlation or coincidence. For example, if you find that both the age of the average driver in Canada and the number of accidents caused by drunk drivers are increasing, you cannot jump to the conclusion that older drivers are the cause of the increase in drunk-driving accidents. Similarly, you must be sure that the result you mention is a genuine product of the event or action.

5. Comparing

One point sometimes forgotten is that comparing things means showing differences as well as similarities—even if the topic does not say "compare and contrast." The easiest method for comparison—though not always the best—is to discuss the first subject in the comparison thoroughly and then move on to the second:

Subject *X:*   Point 1
Point 2
Point 3

Subject *Y:*	Point 1
	Point 2
	Point 3

The problem with this kind of comparison is that it often sounds like two separate essays slapped together. To be successful you must integrate the two subjects, first in your introduction (by putting them both in a single context) and again in your conclusion, where you should bring together the important points you have made about each. When discussing the second subject, try to refer repeatedly to your findings about the first subject ("unlike *X*, *Y* does such and such"). This method may be the wisest choice if the subjects for comparison seem so unlike that it is hard to create similar categories by which to discuss them—if the points you are making about *X* are of a different type than the points you are making about *Y*.

If it is possible to find similar criteria or categories for discussing both subjects, however, the comparison will be more effective if you organize it like this:

Category 1:	Subject *X*
	Subject *Y*
Category 2:	Subject *X*
	Subject *Y*
Category 3:	Subject *X*
	Subject *Y*

Because this kind of comparison is more tightly integrated, the reader can more readily see the similarities and differences between the subjects. As a result, the essay is likely to be more forceful.

Introductions

The beginning of an essay has a dual purpose: to indicate both the topic and your approach to it, and to whet your reader's interest in what you have to say. One effective way of introducing a topic is to place it in a context—to supply a kind of backdrop that will put it in perspective. You step back a pace and discuss the area into which your topic fits, and then gradually lead into your specific field of discussion. Sheridan Baker[1] calls this the funnel approach (see p. 19). For example, suppose that your topic is the growing moral maturity of Brian O'Connal in W.O. Mitchell's *Who Has Seen the Wind?* You might begin with a more general discussion of growing up in the west, or the movement from innocence to experience in other novels. A funnel opening is applicable to almost any kind of essay.

It's a good idea to try to catch your reader's interest right from the start—you know from your own reading how a dull beginning can put you off. The fact that your instructor must read on anyway makes no difference. If a reader has to get through thirty or forty similar essays, it's all the more important for yours to stand out. A funnel opening isn't the only way to catch the reader's attention. Here are three of the most common leads:

The quotation. This approach works especially well when the quotation is taken from the person or work that you will be discussing.

The question. A rhetorical question will only annoy the reader if it's commonplace or the answer is obvious, but a thought-provoking question can make a strong opening. Just be sure that you answer the question in your essay.

The anecdote or telling fact. This is the kind of concrete lead that journalists often use to grab their readers' attention. Save it for your least formal essays—and remember that the incident must really highlight the ideas you are going to discuss.

Whatever your lead, it must relate to your topic: never sacrifice relevance for originality. Finally, whether your introduction is one paragraph or several, make sure that by the end of it your reader clearly knows the direction you are taking.

Conclusions

Endings can be painful—sometimes for the reader as much as for the writer. Too often, the feeling that one ought to say something profound and memorable produces the kind of prose that suggests violins throbbing in the background. You know the sort of thing:

> Clearly the symbolism of Four Quartets is both intellectu-
> ally and emotionally stimulating. Through it Eliot has
> produced poetry of lasting significance which will inspire
> readers for generations to come.

Why is this embarrassing? Because it's phony—a grab-bag of clichés.

Experienced editors often say that many articles and essays would be better without their final paragraphs: in other words, when you have finished what you want to say, the only thing to do is stop. This advice works best for short essays, where you need to keep the central point firmly in the foreground and don't need to remind the reader of it. For longer pieces, where you have developed a number of ideas or a complex line of argument, you should provide a sense of closure.

Readers welcome an ending that helps to tie the ideas together; they don't like to feel they've been left dangling. And since the final impression is often the most lasting, it's in your interest to finish strongly. Simply restating your thesis or summarizing what you have already said isn't forceful enough. What are the other options?

The inverse funnel. The simplest and most basic conclusion is one that restates the thesis *in different words* and then discusses its implications. Sheridan Baker calls this the inverse funnel approach, as opposed to the funnel approach of the opening paragraph.[5]

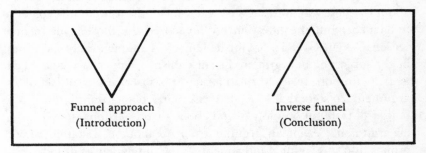

Funnel approach   Inverse funnel
(Introduction)   (Conclusion)

One danger in moving to a wider perspective is that you may try to embrace too much. When a conclusion expands too far it tends to lose focus and turn into an empty cliché, like the conclusion in the preceding example. It's always better to discuss specific implications than to leap into the thin air of vague generalities.

The new angle. A variation of the basic inverse funnel approach is to reintroduce your argument with a new twist. Suggesting some fresh angle can add excitement to your ending. Beware of injecting an entirely new idea, though, or one that's only loosely connected to your original argument: the result could be jarring or even off-topic.

The full circle. If your introduction is based on an anecdote, a question, or a startling fact, you can complete the circle by referring to it again in relation to some of the insights revealed in the main body of your essay.

The stylistic flourish. Some of the most successful conclusions end on a strong stylistic note. Try varying the sentence structure: if most of your sentences are long and complex, make the last one short and punchy, or vice versa. Sometimes you can dramatize your idea with a striking phrase or colourful image. When you are writing your essay, keep your eyes open and your ears tuned for fresh ways of putting things, and save the best for the end.

None of these approaches to endings is exclusive, of course. You may even find that several of them can be combined in a single essay.

The Argumentative Essay

The argumentative essay is particularly common in the humanities. The word "argument" here is used in its precise sense, not in the sense of "dispute" or "controversy", since the purpose of argument is not to win, but to resolve a conflict (whereas the object of persuasion is to win). Thus two medical researchers can engage in an argument about the best way to treat a cancer, since this argument involves a judgement. But the question "Who scored the most goals in one season, Wayne Gretzky or Gordie Howe?" cannot, strictly speaking, be the subject of an argument because the answer is a fact, and a fact is, by definition, true. Nor can a matter of taste be the subject of an argument; to state that "Gretzky is a better player than Howe" is a matter of taste, of opinion — and about such questions there can be no argument. What an argument *can* be about is a statement, or proposition, involving a judgement. If the judgement is disbelieved, then we have an argument.

One of the many ways of conducting an argument properly — that is, with the object of arriving at the truth — is the following four-step procedure:

1. State the subject clearly and fairly, defining any vague or complex terms.
2. State your position about the question, supporting it both by facts and by reasoning from the evidence you have.
3. Refute the arguments against your position, stating them clearly and fairly, and applying to them evidence and reason to show how and why they are wrong.
4. Summarize your argument and emphasize how it has led you to the truth.

Any argument must be based on either evidence or reasoning. There are two kinds of evidence: facts (which we have dealt with above) and authority. By authority as evidence we mean the opinion of someone who is an expert in the field. Thus, with regard to the question about who is the better hockey player, the opinion of someone who has played against both Howe and Gretzky would be of much more weight than the opinion of a casual fan. At the same time, however, the authority of this player is restricted to the subject of professional hockey: his opinion on the problem of abortion, or municipal taxation, would not necessarily be any more authoritative than that of any other citizen. The opinion of a tax lawyer on municipal taxation would be that of an authority, but the lawyer's opinion on hockey players would not necessarily be any more valuable than that of anyone else.

There are three major forms of reasoning:

1. Induction — arriving at a general principle from the observation of particular instances. For example, is it true that young males are poor drivers? Checking the driving records of young males, and comparing them to those of the rest of the population, might lead us to conclude that the general statement is indeed true. That is, from the observation of particular instances we have arrived at a general principle.
2. Deduction — the opposite of induction: young males are, in general, poor drivers, and so it is likely that George, who is only eighteen, is a poor driver. That is, we have applied a general principle to a particular instance.
3. Analogy — a form of comparison: if two things are alike in several ways, they are probably alike in another way too. A common analogy is to compare life to a journey: just as a journey has its freeways and poor back roads, its picnic stops and its accidents, so life has its good and bad stretches, its pleasant times and ugly moments. The danger of using analogies is carrying them so far that they become silly.

Among the most common errors in reasoning are these: the hasty generalization ("all football players are wild boozers", "everybody cheats on income tax"), the false analogy ("a university is like a business, because it all comes down to dollars and cents", "money is like mud; it's no good unless it's spread around"), and begging the question ("Our city council, which is in such poor shape, must be replaced at the next election" — here the "poor shape" of the council must be proven before the rest of the sentence can be accepted). A last error in reasoning is ignoring the question: a prominent actress criticized for her wildly extravagant life will reply by describing the moral upbringing her parents gave her. These kinds of errors are often difficult to recognize, either because they are cleverly concealed or because they are so common that we easily overlook them. But they are all obstacles in argument's attempt to reach the truth.

THE EDITING STAGE

Often the best writer in a class is not the one who can dash off a fluent first draft, but the one who is the best editor. To edit your work well you need to see it as the reader will; you have to distinguish between what you meant to say and what is actually on the page. For this reason it's a good idea to leave some time between drafts, so that when you begin to edit you will be looking at the writing afresh rather than reviewing it from memory. Now's the time to go to a movie or play some squash—do anything that will take your mind off your work. Without this distancing period you can become so involved that it's hard to see your paper objectively.

Editing doesn't mean simply checking your work for errors in grammar or spelling. It means looking at the piece *as a whole* to see if the ideas are (1) well organized, (2) well documented, and (3) well expressed. It may mean adding some paragraphs, deleting others, and shifting still others around. It very likely means adding, deleting, and shifting sentences and phrases. Experienced writers may be able to check several aspects of their work at the same time, but if you are inexperienced or in doubt about your writing, it's best to look at the organization of the ideas before you tackle sentence structure, diction, style, and documentation.

What follows is a check-list of questions to ask yourself as you begin editing. Far from all-inclusive, it focuses on the first step: examining the organization. You probably won't want to check through your work separately for each question: you can group some together and overlook others, depending on your own strengths and weaknesses as a writer.

Preliminary editing check-list

1. Are the purpose and approach of this essay evident from the beginning?
2. Are all sections of the paper relevant to the topic?
3. Is the organization logical?
4. Are the ideas sufficiently developed? Is there enough evidence, explanation, and illustration?
5. Would an educated person who hasn't read the primary material understand everything I'm saying? Should I clarify some parts or add any explanatory material?
6. In presenting my argument, do I take into account opposing arguments or evidence?

7. Do my paragraph divisions give coherence to my ideas? Do I use them to cluster similar ideas and signal changes of idea?
8. Do any parts of the essay seem disjointed? Should I add more transitional words or logical indicators to make the sequence of ideas easier to follow?

Another approach would be to devise your own check-list based on the faults of previous assignments. This is particularly useful when you move from the overview to the close focus on sentence structure, diction, punctuation, spelling, and style. If you have a particular weak area—for example, irrelevant evidence, faulty logic, or run-on sentences—you should give it special attention. Keeping a personal check-list will save you from repeating the same old mistakes.

A few words about appearance

We've all been told not to judge a book by its cover, but the very warning suggests that we have a natural tendency to do so. Readers of essays find the same thing. A well-typed, visually appealing essay creates a receptive reader and, fairly or unfairly, often gets a higher mark than a hand-written one—especially if the hand-writing is messy or hard to read. Whenever possible, therefore, type your essay. If you can't type or afford to hire a typist, take special care that your script is neat and easy to read. If your hand-writing is poor, print. In any case, double-space your lines and leave wide margins on sides, top, and bottom, framing the script in white. Leave three centimetres at least at the sides and top and four centimetres at the bottom, so that the reader has ample space to write comments. Number each page at the top right-hand corner, and provide a neat, well-spaced cover page which includes the title, your name, and the name of your instructor and course. Good looks won't substitute for good thinking, but they will certainly enhance it.

USING A WORD-PROCESSOR

These days it is becoming more common to see student papers with the characteristic type face of the dot matrix or—in rarer cases—laser printer. The advent of the computer and relatively inexpensive, easy-to-use word-processing packages has made a tremendous difference to the way people write. The word-processor can be a wonderful tool to assist you in your writing—if you use it judiciously.

Using a word-processor does not mean "getting into computers";

most word-processing systems simply make your computer keyboard into a fancy typewriter that allows you to correct mistakes before they arrive on paper, rearrange your material for ease of reading, and print out a neat and tidy final copy. Most systems are easy to learn and they can speed up your writing considerably. To some extent they can also help you to improve your writing skills, because they make it easier for you to revise—to add, delete, or correct, change passages, or move paragraphs around. Here are a few simple suggestions that might be useful if you have, or are thinking of getting, a computer to do word-processing.

1. Type your material directly into the computer

The traditional way of writing a paper that eventually will be typed is to write it out in longhand, and then type it or have someone else type it for you. You can speed up the physical writing process enormously by typing your paper directly into the computer. Even if you can't type very well, it doesn't really matter; when you are writing a paper, the time spent thinking will far outweigh the time it takes to enter the words into the computer. A common argument against writing in this fashion is "I can't think at the typewriter." But once you try, you may find it's rewarding. Seeing your thoughts appearing in a legible form in front of you will help keep you going.

2. Try different ways of organizing your paper

Perhaps the most useful aspect of a word-processing system is that it allows you to move blocks of text around so that you can try out different ways of organizing your paper. If you have ever reached the point where your handwritten version has become so complicated that you have to rewrite the whole thing out in order to make any sense of it, you will appreciate being able to make on-screen corrections and rearrangements. You can set up a new organizational structure for your paper and if, after reading it through, you don't like it, you can always go back to your original version.

3. Don't let the system rule your thinking

Seeing something typed out neatly on a screen or on paper makes it seem more acceptable than messy handwriting, even though the quality of the work may be no different. Don't be fooled into thinking that quality typing replaces quality thinking. Read over your work with a critical eye, in the knowledge that you can easily change something that is unsatisfactory. Remember that the word-processor is a tool for you to use—no more than that.

4. Save regularly and back up your files

If you are used to working with a computer, you know the importance of this advice; if not, take it to heart. There is nothing more agonizing than to discover that something has gone wrong and caused you to lose everything you have been working on. It doesn't happen very often, but everyone experiences it at least once, and always unexpectedly. There is one easy way around the problem: when you are writing, save your work file every fifteen minutes or so. Then when your room-mate pulls the plug on the computer to turn on the TV, the most you will lose is the typing you have done since you last saved your file. A potentially more serious problem may arise if your cat decides to find out what computer disks taste like, or if you are careless with a cup of coffee. Again, a little foresight will save you from losing everything. As soon as you have completed a section of work, make a copy of it on another disk and keep it well away from the computer. An up-to-date back-up system like this will spare you a lot of frustration.

Word-processors are not the answer to all your writing needs, but if you are thinking about getting an electric typewriter, you might consider buying an inexpensive computer instead. It will do a lot more for you—and besides, the time spent learning the word-processing function will quickly be surpassed by the time saved in using it.

NOTES

[1]For a more detailed discussion of heuristic procedures, see Richard E. Young, Alton L. Becker, and Kenneth Pike, *Rhetoric, Discovery and Change* (New York: Harcourt Brace Jovanovich, 1970), 119-36.
[2]James McCrimmon, *Writing With a Purpose*, 6th ed. (Boston: Houghton Mifflin Co., 1976), 18.
[3]John R. Trimble, *Writing with Style: Conversations on the Art of Writing* (Englewood Cliffs, N.J.: Prentice-Hall, Inc., 1975), 11.
[4]Sheridan Baker, *The Practical Stylist*, 5th ed. (New York: Harper & Row Pubs. Inc., 1981). 24-5.
[5]*Ibid.*

3
WRITING
a book report

The term *book report* covers a variety of writing assignments, from a simple summary of a book's contents to a sophisticated literary review. In between is the kind that you will most often be asked to produce: an analytic report containing some evaluation. The following guidelines cover the three basic kinds. Before you begin your assignment, be sure to check with your instructor to find out exactly which type is expected.

THE INFORMATIVE BOOK REPORT OR SUMMARY

Your purpose in this kind of report is to summarize a book briefly and coherently. It's not a complicated task, but it does call on your ability to get to the heart of things, to separate what is important from what is not—a useful skill both in school and on the job. Aside from some pertinent publication information, all a simple informative report needs is an accurate summary of the book's contents.

Writing guidelines

Determine the author's purpose

An author writes a book for a reason: to cast some new light on a subject, to propose a new theory, or to bring together the existing knowledge in a field. Whatever the purpose, you have to discover it if you want to understand what guided the author's selection and arrangement of material. The best way to find out what the author intends to do is to check the table of contents, preface, and introduction.

Skim-read the book first

As noted earlier (p. 6), a quick overview of the book's contents will show you what the author considers most important and what kind of evidence he or she presents. The details will be much more understandable once you know where the book as a whole is going.

Reread carefully and take notes

A second, more thorough reading will be the basis of your note-taking. Since you have already determined the relative importance that the author gives to various ideas, you can be selective and avoid getting bogged down in a welter of unimportant detail. Just be sure that you don't neglect any crucial passages or controversial claims.

When you are taking notes try to condense the ideas. Don't take them down word for word, and don't simply paraphrase them. You will have a much firmer grasp of the material if you resist the temptation to quote; force yourself to interpret. This approach will also help to make your report concise—remember, you want to be brief as well as clear. Condensing the material as you take notes will ensure that your report is a true summary, not just a string of quotations or paraphrases.

Pull your notes together to form a clear summary of the contents

Give the same relative emphasis to each area that the author does. Don't just list the topics in the book or the conclusions reached: discriminate between primary ideas and secondary ones.

Follow the book's order of presentation. Strictly speaking, a simple summary need not do so, but it's usually safer to follow the author's lead. That way your summary will be a clear reflection of the original.

Follow the logical chain of the arguments. Don't leave any confusing holes. You won't be able to cover every detail, of course, but you must make sure to trace all the main arguments in such a way that they make logical sense.

Include the key evidence supporting the author's arguments. Without some supporting details, your reader will have no way of assessing the strength of the conclusions.

Tailor the length to fit your needs. A summary can be any length, from one page to six or seven. It depends less on the length of the original material than on your purpose. If the report is an assignment, find out how long your instructor wants it to be. If it's for personal reference only, you will have to decide how much detail you want to have on hand.

Read and revise your report to make sure it's coherent

Summaries can often seem choppy or disconnected because so much of the original is left out. Use linking words and phrases (see p. 82) to help create a flow and give your writing a sense of logical development. Careful paragraph division will also help to frame the various sections of the summary. If the report is for a science or social science course, you can probably use headings as well to identify sections.

Include publication details

Details about the book (publisher, place and date of publication, and number of pages) must appear somewhere in your report, whether at the beginning or at the end. Follow the guidelines in Chapter 11. Separate these publication details from your discussion by a triple space.

THE ANALYTIC BOOK REPORT

An analytic book report—sometimes called a book review—not only summarizes the main ideas in a book but at the same time evaluates them. You are best to begin with an introduction, then follow with your summary and evaluation. Publication details can come either at the beginning or at the end.

Writing guidelines

Introduction

You should provide all the background information necessary for a reader who is not familiar with the book. Here are some of the questions you might consider:
- What is the book about?
- What is the author's purpose? What kind of audience is he or she writing for? How is the topic limited? Is the central theme or argument stated or only implied?
- How does this book relate to others in its special field of interest? To other aspects of the same field?

- What are the author's background and reputation? What other books or articles has he or she written?
- Are there any special circumstances connected with the writing of this book?
- What sources has the author used?

Not all of these questions will be applicable to every book. Nevertheless, an introduction that answers some of them will put your reader in a much better position to appreciate what you have to say.

Summary

Obviously you cannot analyse a book without discussing its contents: the basic steps are the same as for the simple book summary. You may choose to present a condensed version of the book's contents as a separate section, to be followed by your evaluation; or you may prefer to integrate the two, assessing the author's arguments as you present them.

Evaluation

In evaluating the book, you might ask some of the following questions:
- How is the book organized? Are the divisions valid? Does the author give short shrift to certain areas? Is anything left out?
- What kind of assumptions does the author make in presenting the material? Are they stated or implied? Are they valid?
- Does the book accomplish what it sets out to do? Does the author's position change in the course of the book? Are there any contradictions or weak spots in the arguments? Does the author recognize those weaknesses or omissions? Remember that your job is not only to analyse the contents of the book, but to indicate its strengths and weaknesses.
- What kind of evidence is presented to support the author's ideas? Is it reliable and up to date? Are any of the data distorted or misinterpreted? Could the same evidence be used to support a different case? Does the book leave out any important evidence that might weaken its case? Is the author's position convincing?
- Does the author agree or disagree with other writers who have dealt with the same material or problem? In what respects?
- Is the book clearly written and interesting to read? Is the writing repetitious? Too detailed? Not detailed enough? Is the style clear? Or is it plodding, or jargonish, or flippant?

- Does the book raise issues that need further exploration? Does it present any challenges or leave unfinished business for the author or other scholars to pick up?
- To what extent would you recommend this book? What effect has it had on you?

THE LITERARY REVIEW

The literary review is a variation of the analytic book report. Although literature is its most frequent subject, it may deal with a wide range of topics, from art and music to the social sciences. The term "literary" refers to the presentation rather than to the material discussed: the review should stand on its own merit as an attractive piece of writing.

The advantage of a literary review is the freedom it allows you in both content and presentation. You may emphasize any aspect you like, as long as you leave your reader with a basic understanding of what the book is about. In most cases, your purpose is simply to provide a graceful introduction to the work based on a personal assessment of its most intriguing—or annoying—features. Just don't be too personal: some reviewers end up telling us more about themselves than about the book. Although a literary review is usually less comprehensive than an analytic report, it should always be thoughtful, and your judgement must never be superficial.

The best way of learning how to write good literary reviews is to read some of them. Check the book review sections of a magazine such as *Saturday Night*, a journal like *Canadian Forum*, or the weekend edition of the *Globe and Mail* to see different approaches. Pay particular attention to the various techniques that reviewers use to catch the reader's interest and hold it. The basic rule is to reinforce your comments with specific details from the book; concrete examples will add authenticity and life to your review.

4
RESEARCH
in the humanities

The principal research tool of the university student is the library. In order to pursue research efficiently and rapidly, therefore, it is essential that you get to know the library as early as possible. This knowledge is of two kinds: knowledge of what the building contains (location of card and computer catalogues, indexes, periodicals, reading rooms, microfilm and microfiche collections, the general collection of books, photocopiers, journals, reference books, special collections, etc.), and knowledge of the important reference works themselves.

Probably the most efficient method of getting to know the library building and what it contains is to take the guided tour that most university libraries provide for students at the beginning of each academic year. If your library does not provide such a tour, get a map of the library and take your own tour; this will be time well spent and will save you a good deal of trouble later.

Once you know where the various materials are in the library, then you must learn how to use them; it is with such knowledge that this chapter is concerned. In the following chapter, ''Sources in the Humanities'', you will find lists of reference works for each of eighteen different fields in the humanities, with a brief description of each work. The purpose of the present chapter is to briefly describe some of the more general reference works that are relevant either to all of these fields or to a good many of them.

First, however, a few words of caution. You must pay close attention to the title and, especially, to the introductory material of the reference works described below. Although all are easy to use, some of them look extraordinarily complex because they use a special shorthand for references. This shorthand is necessary because of the huge amount of information involved; for instance, *Psychological Abstracts* now publishes the abstracts of more than 40,000 articles annually. However, once you have taken the trouble to understand the method that the reference work uses, finding what you want should be fairly easy.

Note also that, in these descriptions, the expression "fields covered include . . ." is meant only to give you a sample of the work's coverage; it is *not* a list of all the fields that it deals with.

Finally, although the list of reference works below covers a good deal of ground, it is by no means complete. There exist, for the humanities, bibliographies and indexes and collections of abstracts by the thousands. But the works you have here will help you take that crucial first step.

1. BOOK REVIEWS

Book Review Digest (1905—)

A list of book reviews, arranged alphabetically by names of authors of books being reviewed. Includes, for each book reviewed, a summary of the review or quotations from it, as well as an indication of its length. A four-volume cumulated index covers 1905-1974. Deals mainly with popular fiction and non-fiction, but with some scholarly works as well.

An Index to Book Reviews in the Humanities (1960—)

Following the author's name and the title is a list of reviews of each book. Strong coverage of academic and non-fiction books, and international in scope.

Journal of Economic Literature (1963—)

Each quarterly issue includes a long section of book reviews and a list of new books, with a description of the contents of each.

Readers' Guide to Periodical Literature (1900—)

Now in its ninetieth year, the *Guide* is an alphabetical list, by author and subject, of articles published during the year in American and Canadian popular magazines. The last section is a list of book reviews.

2. ABSTRACTS

America: History and Life (1964—)

Abstracts of articles from some 2,000 journals on all aspects of the culture and history of the United States and Canada from prehistoric times to the present. Abstracts are grouped under such headings as the American Colonial Period to 1775, Canada from 1945 to the Present, the Spanish-American War, the Westward Movement and Indian Wars, etc. Each volume includes indexes by subject, by author, and by book reviewed.

Abstracts in Anthropology (1970—)

Published quarterly, these abstracts are taken from nearly one hundred journals, mainly in English. Abstracts are grouped under such headings as Cultural Ecology, Ethnohistory, Minorities, Urban Studies, Fossil Records and Evolution, Sociocultural Change, Kinship, etc. Indexed by author and subject.

Historical Abstracts (1955—)

Multilingual abstracts of books and articles covering all branches of world history from 1450 to the present. Fields include religion, intellectual history, and the history of science, technology, and medicine. Coverage is world-wide except for the United States and Canada, which are to be found in *America: History and Life*.

International Political Science Abstracts (1951—)

Published bimonthly in French and English, this is a collection of abstracts of articles in journals from around the world. Abstracts are grouped under such general headings as Political Science: Method and Theory, Political Thinkers and Ideas, International Relations, National and Area Studies, etc.

Psychological Abstracts (1927—)

Abstracts of articles on all branches of psychology from throughout the world. Abstracts of articles in foreign languages are in English. Published monthly, with annual author and subject indexes. Fields covered include developmental psychology, sport psychology and leisure, psychometrics, communication systems, social psychology, etc.

Sociological Abstracts (1953 —)

Six issues per year, plus a cumulative index issue. Non-evaluative abstracts of international articles on sociology and related disciplines. Abstracts are grouped under such headings as Sociology: History and Theory, Culture and Social Structure, Complex Organizations, Political Interactions, Urban Sociology, etc. Includes indexes by subject, author, and source, as well as a bibliography of book reviews.

Women Studies Abstracts (1972—)

Abstracts of articles grouped under such headings as Sexuality, Family, Family Planning, Abortion, Women's Liberation Movement, Sports and Physical Capabilities, Society and Government, etc. Each four-issue volume includes cumulative author and subject indexes.

3. INDEXES

Art Index (1929 —)

An index of articles in periodicals, arranged by author and subject, but including also yearbooks and museum bulletins. Subjects include architecture, art history, city planning, films, industrial design, interior design, photography, etc. Also includes, at the end, a list of book reviews.

Arts and Humanities Citation Index (1976—)

An annual list, in six volumes, of the most important articles published world-wide in the arts and humanities. Articles can be found by using the citation index (i.e., articles that have referred to an earlier article on the subject), the Permuterm Subject Index (i.e., using key terms), the Corporate Index (i.e., organizations or institutions), and the Source Index (which lists items alphabetically by author).

Canadian Periodical Index (1938 —)

A bilingual list, in all subject areas, of authors of books and articles. Reviews are included under both "Book Reviews" and the name of author reviewed as well as under the author of the review.

Humanities Index (1974 —)

Previously titled the *International Index* (1907-1965) and the *Social Sciences and Humanities Index* (1965-1974), this index is a list, by author and subject, of articles in scholarly journals. Fields covered include philosophy, folklore, history, literature, archaeology, language, performing arts, etc. Includes a long list of book reviews, by subject and by author of book.

Index of Economic Articles (1886 —)

A list, by subject and by author, of articles in 279 economic journals and in collective volumes. Coverage is of publications in English only. Articles appear under such headings as Teaching of Economics, General Economic Theory, Welfare Theory, Social Choice, etc. Indexed by subject and author.

MLA International Bibliography (1919 —)

Published yearly in five volumes by the Modern Language Association, this bibliography lists, within chronological period, and within each period alphabetically by author, books and articles published throughout the world on modern languages, literature, folklore, and linguistics. Volume I deals with literatures in English, Vol. II with European, Asian, African, and South American literatures, Vol. III with Linguistics, Vol. IV with General Literature and Related Topics, and Vol. V with Folklore.

The Music Index (1949 —)

A subject-author guide to articles on music. Over 350 periodicals are covered, representing twenty countries. Includes book reviews, reviews of records and tapes, first performances, and obituaries.

Social Sciences Citation Index (1971 —)

Published annually as a four-part, multi-volume list of the most important literature published world-wide in the social sciences. Articles can be found by using the Citation Index, the Permuterm Subject Index (i.e., key terms), the Corporate Index (i.e., organization or institution), and the Source Index. Covers all the social sciences, including ergonomics, nursing, psychiatry, statistics, women's studies, etc.

Social Sciences Index (1974 —) [See *Humanities Index* for previous titles]

A list, by author and subject, of articles in scholarly journals. Fields covered include anthropology, economics, geography, law and criminology, political science, psychiatry, police science, sociology, etc. At the end is a long list of book reviews, indexed by subject and by author of book.

5
SOURCES
in the humanities

In this chapter you will find lists of some of the principal reference works for eighteen areas in the humanities. Full bibliographical information is given for each book so that you can easily find it in the library or order it for yourself. Although these are all important books, this list is by no means exhaustive; it is meant simply to help you in the first step of finding information about whatever subject interests you in these disciplines. Note also that almost all of these books contain detailed bibliographies of many other sources that will lead you to a more specific and thorough study of your subject.

Each of the several hundred reference titles included in this chapter is followed by a short description of the nature or content of the book. You should pay close attention to these descriptions; although short, they have been made as precise and informative as possible. Keep in mind also that most of the descriptions do *not* repeat information given to you by the title of the book, information that, for a reference text, is always of crucial importance.

You will find, as you work your way through these books, that some of them are valuable as references not just in the humanities but in the sciences as well. This is simply to say that at some points these two areas of human activity have mingled to such an extent that it is difficult to distinguish them. This should not, however, pose a problem for you. Reference books, in whatever field, are your tools; they are there to help you, not to hinder.

Although good research is often difficult, your increasing familiarity with the reference works should make your research increasingly easy, and the results will be ever more enjoyable and intellectually rewarding.

ANTHROPOLOGY

Frantz, Charles. *The Student Anthropologist's Handbook: A Guide to Research, Training, and Career*. Cambridge, Mass.: Schenkman, 1972. Chapters on such topics as becoming an anthropologist, field, lab, and library research, the practising professional, etc.

Gacs, Ute, et al., eds. *Women Anthropologists: A Biographical Dictionary*. New York: Greenwood Press, 1988. Biographies (4-6 pp.) of fifty-eight women anthropologists, mostly American. Each biography is followed by a list of works by and about the scientist.

Hunter, David E., and Phillip Whitten, eds. *Encyclopedia of Anthropology*. New York: Harper and Row, 1976. Some 1400 articles by 100 contributors on the concepts and language of anthropology, its theories, and its leading figures, past and present. Numerous illustrations, charts, and diagrams.

International Bibliography of the Social Sciences: Social and Cultural Anthropology. Vol. 30. London: Tavistock, 1984. Books and articles published during the previous year throughout the world, with English or French translations of work in other languages. A standard work.

Li, Tze-chung. *Social Science Reference Sources: A Practical Guide*. Westport, Conn.: Greenwood Press, 1980. Includes chapters on statistical sources, government publications, data archives, and subdisciplines of the social sciences, such as cultural anthropology, economics, law, political science, etc.

McInnis, Raymond G., and James W. Scott. *Social Science Research Handbook*. New York: Barnes and Noble, 1974. Under Anthropology (pp. 21-33) are found brief critical descriptions of bibliographies, reviews of research, encyclopedias, handbooks, methodological works, linguistics, etc. The second part deals with geographical areas in general and by discipline. Extensive bibliography.

Pearson, Roger. *Anthropological Glossary*. Malabar, Fla.: Robert E. Krieger Publishing, 1985. Definitions, often accompanied by brief descriptions, of several thousand terms (individuals, places, tribes, things, etc).

Press, Jaques Cattell, ed. *American Men and Women of Science*. 14th ed. New York: R.R. Bowker, 1979. 8 vols. Brief biographical entries on some 130,000 scientists working in North America. Each entry includes education, positions held, and field of specialization.

Sills, David L., ed. *International Encyclopedia of the Social Sciences*. New York: The Free Press; London: Collier Macmillan, 1968. 17 vols. A standard work, with vol. 17 the index to the whole. Vol. 18 (1979) contains 215 biographies, with reading lists, of important scientists.

Smith, Margo L., and Yvonne M. Damien, eds. *Anthropological Bibliographies: A Selected Guide*. South Salem, NY: Redgrave Publishing, 1981. A listing, by continent and by sub-area, of more than 3,200 bibliographies, filmographies, and discographies.

Webb, William H., et al. *Sources of Information in the Social Sciences: A Guide to the Literature*. 3rd ed. Chicago: American Library Association, 1986. The section on anthropology (pp. 332-402) is divided in two: a survey of the field (systematic surveys, historical development, method, kinds of anthropology, etc.), and a Survey of the Reference Works (guides, reviews, abstracts, bibliographies by area, periodicals, handbooks, etc.). Each section has a short descriptive introduction.

FILM

Beattie, Eleanor. *The Handbook of Canadian Film*. Toronto: Peter Martin in association with *Take One Magazine*. 2nd ed., 1977. Short entries on individuals and groups in film, native peoples, Third World films, women in film, etc. Bibliography and index.

Cowie, Peter, ed. *International Film Guide*. London: Tantivy Press, 1964 — . An annual surveying the year's films from around the world.

Dyment, Alan R. *The Literature of the Film: A Bibliographical Guide to the Film as Art and Entertainment, 1936-1970*. London: White Lion, 1975. Over 1,300 entries on authors, titles, and subjects, arranged under such headings as history of the screen, personalities, technique, types of film, etc. Each entry is followed by a brief description.

Enser, A.G.S. *Filmed Books and Plays: A List of Books and Plays from Which Films Have Been Made, 1928-1973, Arranged by Names and Topics*. New York: Teachers College Press, 1974. A guide to articles about actors, directors, critics, specific films, etc. Some 5,000 items drawn from 22 film periodicals and 60 more general periodicals.

Halliwell, Leslie. *Halliwell's Filmgoer's Companion*. 8th ed. London: Granada, 1984. Short but lively annotations on films, film companies, actors, themes, etc.

Hubbard, Linda S., and Owen O'Donnell, eds. *Contemporary Theatre, Film, and Television*. Detroit: Gale, 1984-1989. 7 vols. Sub-title: "A Biographical Guide Featuring Performers, Directors, Writers, Producers, Designers, Managers, Choreographers, Technicians, Composers, Executives, Dancers, and Critics in the United States and Great Britain".

International Motion Picture Almanac. Richard Gertner, ed. New York: Quigley, 1929 — . Annual record of awards and polls, who's who, statistics, films, distributors, theatre circuits, the world market, etc.

Rehrauer, George. *Cinema Booklist*. Metuchen, NJ: Scarecrow Press, 1972. Supplement One, 1974; Supplement Two, 1977. The three volumes list some 4,000 books on films, with detailed comments on each.

Roud, Richard, ed. *Cinema: A Critical Dictionary*. New York: Viking, 1980. 2 vols. Detailed discussions, by some 40 critics, of directors and their films, and of a few actors.

Samples, Gordon. *How To Locate Reviews of Plays and Films. A Bibliography of Criticism from the Beginnings to the Present*. Metuchen, NJ: Scarecrow Press, 1976. Annotated entries on the medieval stage, silent and experimental film, the baroque stage, Pulitzer Prize plays, Irish theatre, etc.

Schuster, Mel, comp. *Motion Picture Directors: A Bibliography of Magazine and Periodical Articles, 1900-1972*. Metuchen, NJ: Scarecrow Press, 1973. Articles listed from 340 publications covering more than 2,000 directors, filmmakers, and animators.

FOLKLORE

Brunvand, Jan Harold. *Folklore: A Study and Research Guide*. New York: St Martin's Press, 1976. An annotated guide to the most important works concerning folklore theories and leading scholars past and present, as well as biographies, serials, textbooks, folklore genres, etc. The final chapter deals with preparing and writing a research paper on folklore.

Cotterell, Arthur. *A Dictionary of World Mythology*. Oxford: Oxford University Press, 1986. Entries on figures and countries from around the world. Detailed index.

Dorson, Richard M., ed. *Handbook of American Folklore*. Bloomington: Indiana University Press, 1983. Over 60 chapters by different scholars on topics such as "Afro-American Folk Music", "Rags to Riches", "Using Video in the Field", "Filming the Folk", "Factory Folklore", "Bibliographies and Indexes in American Folklore Research", etc.

Fowke, Edith, and Carole H. Carpenter. *Explorations in Canadian Folklore*. Toronto: McClelland and Stewart, 1985. Chapters, by various experts, on such topics as Inuit music, ballad singing in Nova Scotia, Paul Bunyan, folk medicine in French Canada, ethnic jokes, etc.

_____. *A Bibliography of Canadian Folklore in English*. Toronto: University of Toronto Press, 1981. A list of over 3,700 books, articles, films, and records, presenting either authentic material or secondary works.

Frazer, J.G. *The New Golden Bough*, ed. Theodor H. Gaster. New York: S.G. Phillips, 1968. A condensation of Frazer's twelve-volume work, a classical study of magic and religion.

Grimal, Pierre, ed. *Larousse World Mythology*. New York: G.P. Putnam's Sons, 1965. Chapters on all parts of the world, including Greece, Rome, Persia, Celtic Lands, Eskimo Lands, Germanic Lands, etc. Profusely illustrated.

Leach, Maria, ed. *Standard Dictionary of Folklore, Mythology and Legend*. San Francisco: Harper and Row, 1972. Thousands of entries (some quite detailed) on gods, folk heroes, dances, ballads, the folklore of animals and plants, games, riddles, witchcraft, omens, etc.

Mercatante, Anthony S. *The Facts on File Encyclopedia of World Mythology and Legend*. New York: Facts on File, 1988. Over 3,000 entries on mythology and legend from around the world, and from earliest times to the present. Numerous illustrations, and bibliography.

Senior, Michael. *The Illustrated Who's Who in Mythology*. London: Orbis, 1985. Several hundred brief entries on important mythological figures from around the world and from earliest times.

South, Malcolm, ed. *Mythical and Fabulous Creatures: A Source Book and Research Guide*. New York: Greenwood Press, 1987. Individual chapters, with bibliography, on the unicorn, the dragon, the phoenix, the griffin, the vampire, sirens, harpies, etc.

HISTORY

A. Canadian

The Canadian Encyclopedia. James H. Marsh, ed. in chief. 2nd ed. Edmonton: Hurtig, 1988. 4 vols. Over 2,000 authorities contributed to this most recent of Canadian encyclopedias. Vol. 4 contains an index to the whole.

Cardinal, Claudette. *The History of Quebec: A Bibliography of Works in English.* Concordia University: Centre for the Study of Anglophone Quebec, 1981. A list of over 3,400 books and articles dealing with the history of Quebec up to 1976.

Careless, J.M.S. *Canada: A Story of Challenge.* 3rd ed. Toronto: Macmillan, 1970. Chapters on geographical influences, New France, the American Revolution, the forces leading to Confederation, Canada and the two world wars, etc.

Creighton, Donald. *Canada's First Century: 1867-1967.* Toronto: Macmillan, 1970. Includes such chapters as "Confederation and Expansion", "The End of Colonial Security", "The Mackenzie King Millenium", "Obscure Destiny", etc.

————. *A History of Canada: Dominion of the North.* Revised and enlarged ed. Cambridge, Mass.: Riverside, 1958. A standard work.

Dictionary of Canadian Biography. Francess G. Halpenny, general ed. Vol. XI: 1881-1890. Toronto: University of Toronto Press, 1982. Vol. I (1966) dealt with persons of Canadian interest who died between 1000 and 1700; subsequent volumes bring coverage up to 1890. Also published in French by Les Presses de l'Université Laval. The standard work of Canadian biography.

Finlay, J.L., and D.N. Sprague. *The Structure of Canadian History.* Scarborough, Ont.: Prentice-Hall Canada, 3rd ed., 1989. Extremely detailed; bibliography follows each of 28 chapters. Included in appendices are The British North America Act (1867) and The Constitution Act (1982).

Lower, Arthur R.M. *Colony to Nation: A History of Canada.* Toronto: Longman, Green, 2nd ed., 1947. A classic work of Canadian history.

A Reader's Guide to Canadian History. Vol. 1: *Beginnings to Confederation.* D.A. Muise, ed. Vol. 2: *Confederation to the Present.* J.L. Granatstein and Paul Stevens, eds. Toronto: University of Toronto Press, 1982. Discussions of the most recent research in the major areas of Canadian historical writing. Topics include foreign and defence policy, economic and business history, social and intellectual history, and a section on each geographical area of Canada.

Shortt, Adam, and Arthur G. Doughty, general eds. *Canada and its Provinces: A History of the Canadian People and their Institutions by One Hundred Associates*. Toronto: Publishers' Association of Canada, 1913-1917. 23 vols. Extremely detailed survey of Canadian history. Vol. 23 is an index to the whole work.

Smith, Dwight L., ed. *The History of Canada: An Annotated Bibliography*. Santa Barbara, Cal.: American Bibliographical Center — Clio Press, 1983. An annotated bibliography of 3,300 articles from 2,000 periodicals in 42 languages, published between 1973 and 1978.

Thibault, Claude. *Bibliographia Canadiana*. Don Mills, Ont.: Longman Canada, 1973. A bibliography of Canadian historical literature, listing over 25,000 books and articles.

Who's Who in Canada, 1988. Toronto: Global Press, 1988. Biographies of over 700 important Canadians from all walks of life. Published annually since 1906.

B. American

Concise Dictionary of American History. Wayne Andrews, ed. New York: Charles Scribner's Sons, 1962. Over 100 scholars have written several thousand entries on individuals, groups, places, events, institutions, documents, etc. A concise version of the original six-volume work (below).

Dictionary of American Biography. New York: Charles Scribner's Sons, 1928-1936. 20 vols. Supplement 7 (1961-1965): 1981. The standard work on American biography. With the publication, in 1981, of Supplement 7, coverage has now been extended to those persons who died up to the end of 1965. Over 17,000 biographies have now been published.

Dictionary of American History. James Truslow Adams et al., eds. New York: Charles Scribner's Sons, 1961. 6 vols. Index, 1963. Over 5,000 articles on all aspects of American history.

Encyclopedia of American Facts and Dates. Gorton Carruth et al., eds. New York: Thomas Y. Crowell, 1972. List of facts, dates, and events in American history, from earliest times to the present, in chronological order. Divided into four fields of interest, in four columns, on facing pages.

Freidel, Frank, ed. *Harvard Guide to American History*. Cambridge, Mass.: Belknap Press of Harvard University Press, 1974. 2 vols. Exhaustive bibliography of books and articles on all aspects of American history since the beginnings. No annotations.

Johnson, Thomas H. *The Oxford Companion to American History*. New York: Oxford University Press, 1966. Articles on "lives, events, and places significant in the founding and growth of the nation".

Library of Congress. *A Guide to the Study of the United States of America: Representative Books Reflecting the Development of American Life and Thought*. Washington, DC: Library of Congress, 1960. Under such headings as Literature, The American Indian, Geography, Language,Medicine and Public Health, Entertainment, Military History, Land and Agriculture, etc., the compilers provide brief biographies and annotations of important works in all fields.

Webster's Guide to American History: A Chronological, Geographical, and Biographical Survey and Compendium. Springfield, Mass.: G. and C. Merriam Co., 1971. From Columbus to the present, including sections on the revolution, Canada and Mexico, population, the city, etc. Maps, tables, illustrations, and biographies of more than 1,000 notable Americans.

Who's Who in American Politics, 1987-88. 11th ed. New York: R.R. Bowker, 1987. Published annually since 1967. Brief biographies of over 23,000 politically active men and women, from the president, through cabinet members, senators, governors, national and state party chairs, to minor party officials and small-town mayors.

Writings on American History 1985-86: A Subject Bibliography of Articles. Cecelia J. Dadian, ed. Washington, DC: American Historical Association, 1987. Published annually since 1902, this book lists a large number of articles on all aspects of American life. Some of the earlier volumes also include books. No annotations.

C. British

Barzun, Jacques, and Henry F. Graff. *The Modern Researcher*. 3rd ed. New York: Harcourt, Brace, Jovanovich, 1977. Includes chapters on techniques of research, finding and verifying facts, handling ideas, bias, organizing papers, etc.

British Political Facts, 1900-1985. David Butler and Gareth Butler, eds. New York: St Martin's Press, 1986. Lists of ministries, prime ministers, shadow cabinets, party conferences, election results, unions, etc.

The Cambridge History of the British Empire. Cambridge: Cambridge University Press, 1929-1963. 8 vols. Extremely detailed study of British expansion and imperial policy. Vol. 6 (1930) deals with Canada and Newfoundland. Extensive bibliography and index in each volume.

Cook, Chris, and John Stevenson. *The Longman's Handbook of Modern British History*. 2nd ed. London: Longman, 1988. Genealogical charts, prices and wages, coal output, unemployment, treaties, religion, etc., all illustrated by numerous chronologies.

A Dictionary of British History. J.P. Kenyon, editorial consultant. London: Secker and Warburg, 1981. Some 3,000 brief entries on British political and social events, people, foreign affairs, scientific developments, etc., from the Roman conquest to 1970.

The Dictionary of National Biography, 1961-1970. E.T. Williams and C.S. Nicholls, eds. Oxford: Oxford University Press, 1981. First published in 1908, the DNB (now in 21 volumes and supplements) is the standard source of biographical information for British subjects who died between earliest times and 1970.

Handbook of British Chronology. E.G. Fryde et al., eds. London: Royal Historical Society, 1986. Chronologies of rulers of Scotland, bishops of Ireland and England, chancellors of Scotland, admirals of England, secretaries of state for the colonies, etc.

The Oxford History of England. Sir George Clark, ed. Oxford: Clarendon Press, 1937 — . Sixteen volumes have so far been published in this standard work.

Poulton, Helen J. *The Historian's Handbook: A Descriptive Guide to Reference Works*. Norman: University of Oklahoma Press, 1972. Annotated guide to directories of newspapers and serials, legal

sources, government publications, bibliographies of history, encyclopedias, etc.

Ridley, Jasper. *The History of England*. London: Routledge and Kegan
Paul, 1981. A rapid survey from the fifth century to 1979.

Roebuck, Janet. *The Making of Modern English Society from 1850*. New
York: Charles Scribner's Sons, 1973. Includes chapters on English
social classes in the nineteenth century, the First World War, the
welfare state, society in the 1940s, etc.

Trevelyan, G.M. *English Social History: A Survey of Six Centuries, Chaucer
to Queen Victoria*. 3rd ed. London: Longmans, Green and Co., 1946.
The English people described in detail by an eminent historian.

LITERATURE

A. Canadian

Atwood, Margaret. *Survival: A Thematic Guide to Canadian Literature*.
Toronto: Anansi, 1972. Not a survey, but an outline of key patterns,
such as "Nature the Monster", "Ancestral Totems", "Quebec:
Burning Mansions", and "Jail-Breaks and Recreations", etc.

Canadian Writers and Their Works. Robert Lecker et al., eds. Toronto:
ECW Press, 1988-1989. 10 vols. A 20-volume collection, eventually,
of critical essays covering Canadian fiction and poetry over the past
two centuries. Each essay (4-7 per volume, 30-60 pages per essay)
deals with the writer's life and work. Bibliographies of primary works
and criticism.

Gnarowski, Michael. *A Concise Bibliography of English-Canadian Literature*. Rev. ed. Toronto: McClelland and Stewart, 1978. A selective
checklist of both primary works (alphabetically by author) and critical
books and articles, from the 18th century to the 1970s.

Klinck, Carl F., et al., eds. *Literary History of Canada*. 2nd ed. Toronto:
University of Toronto Press, 1976. 3 vols. The standard history of
Canadian literature written in English. Volume 4, edited by Carl
Berger et al., was published in 1990.

Lecker, Robert, and Jack David, eds. *The Annotated Bibliography of
Canada's Major Authors*. Downsview, Ont.: ECW Press, 1979-1989.
Seven volumes published so far in this ongoing series. Each volume

is devoted to four or five authors, with a list of each author's works, and an extensive, annotated list of reviews and critical works.

Moss, John. *A Reader's Guide to the Canadian Novel*. 2nd ed. Toronto: McClelland and Stewart, 1987. Critical commentaries on novels by 469 writers, including Québécois novels in translation and novels for young readers. Appendices on chronology, primary setting, types of novels.

Moyles, R.G. *English-Canadian Literature to 1900: A Guide to Information Sources*. Detroit: Gale, 1976. A list of the important works written by Canadian authors before 1900, and criticism of these works up to 1973. Also includes general reference guides and literary histories and criticism.

Pacey, Desmond. *Creative Writing in Canada: A Short History of English-Canadian Literature*. Toronto: Ryerson, 1961. First published in 1952, this is an early standard survey, dealing with works from 1750 to the 1950s.

Toye, William, gen. ed. *The Oxford Companion to Canadian Literature*. Toronto: Oxford University Press, 1983. Articles, in alphabetical order, mainly on genres and authors (English and French), but also including history, sociology, and politics.

Waterston, Elizabeth. *Survey: A Short History of Canadian Literature*. Toronto: Methuen, 1973. Includes reading lists. The "Survey Chart" at the end shows, in three parallel columns, a Canadian historical chronology and major literary events in Canada and elsewhere.

Watters, Reginald Eyre. *A Checklist of Canadian Literature and Background Materials: 1628-1960*. 2nd ed. Toronto: University of Toronto Press, 1972. Records all known titles produced by English-speaking Canadians up to 1960.

Woodcock, George, ed. *The Canadian Novel in the Twentieth Century*. Toronto: McClelland and Stewart, 1975. Critical essays on major novelists and their works.

B. American

Abel, Darrel. *American Literature*. Woodbury, NY: Barron's Educational Series, 1963. 3 vols. Detailed descriptions and critical analyses of writings from the Puritans to the end of the nineteenth century.

Vol. 4, *Recent American Literature*, by Donald Heiney (1958), covers the twentieth century up to the mid-1950s.

Bigsby, C.W.E. *A Critical Introduction to Twentieth-Century American Drama*. Cambridge: Cambridge University Press, 1982-1985. 3 vols. Concentrates on the major playwrights and theatre groups. Extensive notes and indexes.

Gohdes, Clarence, and Sanford E. Marovitz. *Bibliographical Guide to the Study of the Literature of the U.S.A.* 5th ed. Durham, NC: Duke University Press, 1984. In addition to sections on literature, includes literary terms, American history, magazines and newspapers, the book trade, women's studies, philosophy, religion, etc.

Hart, James D. *The Oxford Companion to American Literature*. 5th ed. New York: Oxford University Press, 1983. Thousands of alphabetically arranged entries on authors, novels, plays, poems, biographies, literary movements, newspapers, printers, etc.

Hoffman, Daniel, ed. *Harvard Guide to Contemporary American Writing*. Cambridge, Mass.: Belknap Press of Harvard University Press, 1979. A critical survey of American poetry, fiction, drama, and criticism from 1945 to the end of the 1970s.

Hubbell, Jay B., et al. *Eight American Authors: A Review of Research and Criticism*. New York: W.W. Norton, 1963. Extensive survey of bibliographies, editions, biographies, and criticism of Poe, Emerson, Hawthorne, Thoreau, Melville, Whitman, Twain, and James.

Karl, Frederick R. *American Fictions, 1940/1980: A Comprehensive History and Critical Evaluation*. New York: Harper and Row, 1983. An exhaustive survey of American fiction since 1940. Detailed index to hundreds of writers and books.

Kuntz, Joseph M. *Poetry Explication: A Checklist of Interpretation Since 1925 of British and American Poems Past and Present*. Rev. ed. Denver, Col.: Allan Swallow, 1962. Poets, from Chaucer to the 1950s, are listed alphabetically. Under each is a brief list of articles that explain individual works. Books are excluded.

Leary, Lewis. *American Literature: A Study and Research Guide*. New York: St Martin's Press, 1976. Includes chapters on literary histories, types and schools of criticism, bibliographical guides, biographical sources, and separate sections on 29 major writers. A final chapter deals with the research paper.

Palmer, Helen H., and Jane Anne Dyson. *American Drama Criticism: Interpretations, 1890-1965 inclusive, of American Drama Since the First Play Produced in America*. Hamden, Conn.: The Shoe String Press, 1967. Critical books and articles on more than 300 plays.

Spiller, Robert E., et al., eds. *Literary History of the United States*. 4th ed. New York: Macmillan, 1974. 2 vols. Vol. I is a survey of all American literature from colonial times to the 1960s; vol. II is an exhaustive bibliography of authors, movements, and background. A standard work.

Stauffer, Donald Barlow. *A Short History of American Poetry*. New York: E.P. Dutton, 1974. A survey of the major writers and periods from the beginnings to the 1960s. Includes a bibliography for each chapter.

C. English

Baugh, Albert C., ed. *A Literary History of England*. 2nd ed. New York: Appleton-Century-Crofts, 1967. A standard one-volume survey. Extensive bibliographies and index.

Daiches, David. *A Critical History of English Literature*. New York: Ronald Press, 1960. 2 vols. A survey from Anglo-Saxon literature to the early part of the twentieth century. Vol. 2 contains an index to some 1,300 authors and works.

Drabble, Margaret, ed. *The Oxford Companion to English Literature*. 5th ed. Oxford: Oxford University Press, 1985. Thousands of alphabetically arranged entries on English authors, individual works, literary societies, British and Irish mythology, coffee houses, publishers, booksellers, newspapers, literary agents, literary and artistic movements, etc.

Ford, Boris, ed. *The New Pelican Guide to English Literature*. 3rd ed. Harmondsworth: Penguin, 1982-83. 8 vols. A detailed survey from Chaucer to the 1970s. Extensive bibliography in each volume.

Kennedy, Arthur G., and Donald B. Sands. *A Concise Bibliography for Students of English*. 5th ed. Stanford, Cal.: Stanford University Press, 1972. Chapters on bibliographical guides, periodicals, reference works, language, literature by both periods and by forms and types, the profession, etc.

Kuntz, Joseph M. *Poetry Explication: A Checklist of Interpretation Since 1925 of British and American Poems Past and Present*. Rev. ed. Denver, Col.: Allan Swallow, 1962. Poets, from Chaucer to the 1950s, are listed alphabetically. Under each is a brief list of articles that explain individual works. Books are excluded.

The Oxford History of English Literature. Oxford: Clarendon Press, 1945-1989. 14 vols. An extensive, scholarly survey of English literature from earliest times. Lengthy annotated bibliographies in most volumes.

Palmer, Helen H., and Anne Jane Dyson. *English Novel Explication: Criticisms to 1972*. London: Clive Bingley, 1973. A bibliography of books and articles on the works of more than 120 novelists. A complement to Inglis F. Bell and Donald Baird, *The English Novel, 1578-1956: Checklist of Twentieth Century Criticisms* (Denver, Col.: Swallow, 1959), which covered criticism published up to 1957.

Preminger, Alex, ed. *Princeton Encyclopedia of Poetry and Poetics*. Enlarged ed. Princeton, NJ: Princeton University Press, 1974. Some 1,000 entries on all aspects of poetry, including theory, technique, and criticism, from earliest times to the 1970s. Numerous bibliographies. A standard work.

Stevenson, Lionel. *The English Novel: A Panorama*. Boston: Houghton Mifflin, 1960. A detailed survey, from before 1600 to the mid-twentieth century. Includes bibliographies for each chapter and a chronological summary of novels from 1581 to the 1950s.

Watson, George, ed. *The Concise Cambridge Bibliography of English Literature: 600-1950*. 2nd ed. Cambridge: Cambridge University Press, 1965. Under each section, from the Old English Period to the Early Twentieth Century, entries are arranged under such headings as Bibliography, Literary History, Collections and Anthologies, Grammars and Dictionaries, and Authors.

D. French-Canadian

Brazeau, J. Raymond. *An Outline of Contemporary French Canadian Literature*. Toronto: Forum House, 1972. A short introduction to the background of French-Canadian literature in the nineteenth and twentieth centuries, with bibliography, followed by a thematic study of ten major authors, including Roy, Thériault, Bessette, Hébert, Aquin, Blais, etc.

Cagnon, Maurice. *The French Novel of Quebec.* Boston: Twayne, 1986. A chronological survey of the Quebec novel, emphasizing the nineteenth and twentieth centuries. The bibliography of works by the novelists includes translations; there is also a bibliography of critical works.

Cotnam, Jacques. *Contemporary Quebec: An Analytical Bibliography.* Toronto: McClelland and Stewart, 1973. A list, in French and English, of bibliographies and biographical dictionaries, as well as of works dealing with culture, history, literature, religion, nationalism, etc.

Fee, Margery, and Ruth Cawker. *Canadian Fiction: An Annotated Bibliography.* Toronto: Peter Martin Associates, 1976. Brief summaries of Canadian novels in English and of those in French which have been translated. Includes title index, subject guide, and annotations of short-story anthologies.

Lochhead, Douglas. *Bibliography of Canadian Bibliographies / Bibliographie des bibliographies canadiennes.* 2nd ed. Toronto: University of Toronto Press, 1972. An alphabetical list, by author, in both French and English, of bibliographies on all aspects of· Canadian life. Includes an extensive subject index.

Stratford, Philip. *Bibliography of Canadian Books in Translation: French to English and English to French.* Ottawa: Humanities Research Council of Canada, 1977. Includes translations of fiction, poetry, and drama, as well as of travel journals, essays, religion, etc.

Sutherland, Ronald. *The New Hero: Essays in Comparative Quebec/Canadian Literature.* Toronto: Macmillan, 1977. Essays in English on both French and English novelists and poets. Includes bibliography of French-Canadian novels translated into English.

Tougas, Gérard. *History of French-Canadian Literature.* Alta Lind Cook, trans. 2nd ed. Toronto: Ryerson, 1966. A critical survey from the beginnings in the eighteenth century to the early 1960s.

Urbas, Jeannette. *From Thirty Acres to Modern Times: The Story of French-Canadian Literature.* Toronto: McGraw-Hill Ryerson, 1976. Includes sections on Rural Myths and Fidelity to the Soil, Urban Social Problems, Modern Times: Keynote for Change, etc.

Warwick, Jack. *The Long Journey: Literary Themes of French Canada*. Toronto: University of Toronto Press, 1968. An analysis of such major themes as empire, quest, regeneration, revolt, etc.

E. French

Brée, Germaine. *Twentieth-Century French Literature*. Louise Guiney, trans. Chicago: University of Chicago Press, 1983. A detailed critical history. Includes bibliography and "French Journals and Reviews Published between 1920 and 1970".

Cabeen, D.C., gen. ed. *A Critical Bibliography of French Literature*. [Syracuse, N.Y.]: Syracuse University Press, 1947-1980. 6 vols. An annotated bibliography covering schools and movements as well as individual writers, from the medieval period to the 1970s.

Cruickshank, John. *French Literature and Its Background*. 6 vols. London: Oxford University Press, 1968-1970. A survey from the sixteenth century (vol. 1) to the twentieth (vol. 6). Each volume includes an extensive chronological table.

Dictionary of Literary Biography. Detroit: Gale. Three volumes have so far appeared that are relevant to French studies: *French Novelists, 1900-1930* (vol. 65, 1988), *1930-1960* (vol. 72, 1988), and *Since 1960* (vol. 83, 1989). Biographies run from ten to twenty-five pages, and each includes a list of works by and about the writer.

Fowlie, Wallace. *French Literature: Its History and Its Meaning*. Englewood Cliffs, NJ: Prentice-Hall, 1973. A brief survey, from the Middle Ages to 1970, of the principal writers and movements.

Mercier, Vivian. *A Reader's Guide to the New Novel: From Queneau to Pinget*. New York: Farrar, Straus and Giroux, 1971. A survey of the New Novel, followed by detailed study of seven of the principal novelists. Bibliography of works by and about each writer.

Osburn, Charles B. *Research and Reference Guide to French Studies*. 2nd ed. Metuchen, NJ: Scarecrow Press, 1981. A list of some 6,000 titles, in both French and English, of literary and language dictionaries, bibliographies, background works, and critical studies of the principal genres, from earliest times to the 1970s.

Peyre, Henri. *What Is Romanticism?* Roda Roberts, trans. University, Alabama: University of Alabama Press, 1977. The nature of romanticism in Western Europe, with emphasis on France.

Reid, Joyce M.H., ed. *The Concise Oxford Dictionary of French Literature.* Oxford: Clarendon Press, 1976. Thousands of descriptive entries on writers, works, places, schools, types of criticism, etc. An abridgement of the *Oxford Companion to French Literature.*

Saisselin, Rémy G. *The Rule of Reason and the Ruses of the Heart: A Philosophical Dictionary of Classical French Criticism, Critics, and Aesthetic Issues.* Cleveland: The Press of Case Western Reserve University, 1970. Detailed entries on seventeenth-century interpretations of such important terms as Academy, Ancients and Moderns, Eclogue or Idyll, Pantomime, Sublime, etc. Part II is a series of biographical and bibliographical articles on twenty major authors, from d'Alembert to Voltaire.

MUSIC

Brockman, William S. *Music: A Guide to the Reference Literature.* Littleton, Col.: Libraries Unlimited, 1987. Detailed annotations on histories, directories, bibliographies of music, music literature, and individual musicians, specialized and subject discographies, current periodicals, etc.

Cohen, Aaron I. *International Encyclopedia of Women Composers.* New York and London: Books & Music (USA), 1987. 2 vols. Thousands of brief biographies of women composers throughout the world, and from ancient times to the present. Numerous appendixes in vol. 2 on composers by country and century, list of pseudonyms, international music societies, etc.

Duckles, Vincent, comp. *Music Reference and Research Materials: An Annotated Bibliography.* 3rd ed. New York: The Free Press, 1974. Thousands of entries on histories of music, encyclopedias, catalogues of music libraries, discographies, directories, etc. Indexes of authors, subjects, and titles.

Holoman, D. Kern. *Writing about Music: A Style Sheet from the Editors of* 19th-Century Music. Berkeley: University of California Press, 1988. How to deal with music terminology, citations, musical examples, concert programs, etc.

International Who's Who in Music and Musicians' Directory. 11th ed. Cambridge: Melrose Press, 1988. In addition to the biographies of over 6,000 performers, composers, and conductors, there are appendixes on orchestras, major competitions and awards, music libraries, etc.

Kennedy, Michael. *The Oxford Dictionary of Music*. Oxford: Oxford University Press, 1985. Entries on operas, composers, places, instruments, festivals, poems set to music, universities, organ builders, jazz-band leaders, hymns, etc.

Marco, Guy A. *Information on Music: A Handbook of Reference Sources in European Languages*. 3 vols. Littleton, Col.: Libraries Unlimited, 1975-1984. Vol. 1 lists dictionaries of terms, principal histories, bibliographies, reviews, thematic indexes, discographies, etc.; vol. 2 deals with the Americas; and vol. 3 with Europe.

The Music Index: A Subject-Author Guide to Music Periodical Literature. Warren, Mich.: Harmonie Park Press. *The Music Index*, published monthly since 1949, is an alphabetically arranged list of current performances, book reviews, books, music and record reviews, etc.

Picerno, Vincent J. *Dictionary of Musical Terms*. Brooklyn, NY: Haskell House, 1976. Brief definitions, often with explanations, of several thousand musical terms. Numerous drawings and diagrams.

Sadie, Stanley, ed. *The New Grove Dictionary of Music and Musicians*. 20 vols. London: Macmillan, 1980. Over 22,000 entries on instruments and their makers, composers, performers, musical genres and forms, theory and composition, terminology, etc., from earliest times to the 1970s. The standard work in English.

Winesanker, Michael, comp. *Books on Music: A Classified List*. Texas Association of Music Schools, 1979. Part A deals with the literature about music (histories, biographies, instruments, vocal music, etc.), and Part B with musical instruction and study.

PHILOSOPHY

Bynagle, Hans E. *Philosophy: A Guide to the Reference Literature*. Littleton, Col.: Libraries Unlimited, Inc., 1986. Includes sections on dictionaries, encyclopedias, and handbooks, both general and specialized; indexes, abstracts, and journals; general and specialized bibliographies; core journals; etc.

Copleston, Frederick, S.J. *A History of Philosophy*. London: Burns
Oates and Washbourne, and Search Press, 1946-1975. 9 vols. A
standard history, with extensive bibliographies in the later volumes.

Directory of American Philosophers: 1986-87. Archie J. Bahm, ed. Bowling Green, Ohio: Philosophy Documentation Center, 1986. Lists,
for the US and Canada, of philosophers, university philosophy
departments, publishers, journals, etc. Companion volume to the
International Directory of Philosophy and Philosophers.

The Encyclopedia of Philosophy. Paul Edwards, ed. in chief. New York:
Macmillan, 1967. 8 vols. Some 1,500 articles deal with Eastern and
Western philosophy, from ancient to modern times. A bibliography
follows each article, and an index to the entire work is at the end of
vol. 8.

Gorovitz, Samuel, et al. *Philosophical Analysis: An Introduction to Its
Language and Techniques*. 2nd ed. New York: Random House, 1969.
Includes sections on elementary logic, assertions and propositions,
the divisions of philosophy, reading and writing philosophy, etc.

Lacey, A.R. *A Dictionary of Philosophy*. 2nd ed. London: Routledge
and Kegan Paul, 1986. A layman's guide to some of the most common terms in philosophy. Numerous bibliographies.

Magill, Frank N., ed. *World Philosophy: Essay-Reviews of 225 Major
Works*. 5 vols. Englewood Cliffs, NJ: Salem Press, 1982. Each essay
on a major work is followed by a summary of two or three important
books/articles on the work, and a brief annotated list of recommended
readings.

*The Philosopher's Index: An International Index to Philosophical Periodicals
and Books*. Bowling Green, Ohio: Philosophy Documentation Center,
1987. Includes a subject index of articles published from around the
world, abstracts of articles, and an index of book reviews. Published
quarterly, with annual cumulations.

Tice, Terrence N., and Thomas P. Slavens. *Research Guide to Philosophy*. Chicago: American Library Association, 1983. Overviews of the
principal philosophers and areas of philosophy, from earliest times to
the present. The final section is an annotated list of reference works.

Turner, Roland, ed. *Thinkers of the Twentieth Century*, 2nd ed. Chicago:
St James Press, 1987. Brief biographies of over 450 thinkers and lists

of their principal works, followed by a brief list of critical works on each thinker and a critical essay.

Urmson, J.O., ed. *The Concise Encyclopedia of Western Philosophy and Philosophers*. 2nd ed. London: Hutchinson, 1975. Brief entries on philosophers and ideas.

POLITICAL SCIENCE

A Bibliography for Students of Politics. Oxford: Oxford University Press, 1971. Sections on political institutions, theory of politics, international relations, modern social institutions, the political structure of the Commonwealth, etc. Emphasis especially on Britain and the U.S.

Day, Alan J., ed. *Political Parties of the World*. 3rd ed. Chicago: St James Press, 1988. Brief descriptions of all political parties in each country, including history, leaders, orientation, addresses, etc.

East, Roger, ed. *Keesing's Contemporary Archives: Record of World Events*. London: Longman, 1983 — . A monthly compilation of political and economic news, including statistics, from around the world.

Holler, Frederick L. *Information Sources of Political Science*. 3rd ed. Santa Barbara, Cal.: ABC-Clio, 1981. A guidebook to reference sources for the social sciences, American government and politics, international relations, political theory, etc. World-wide scope but American emphasis.

International Bibliography of the Social Sciences: Vol. 34: *Political Science*. London: Routledge, 1988. Published annually since 1952 in four volumes (with the other volumes dedicated to Sociology, Economics, and Social and Cultural Anthropology), this extensive work covers the world.

International Political Science Abstracts/Documentation Politique Internationale. Paris: International Political Science Association/Association Internationale de Science Politique, 1951 — . Provides non-evaluative abstracts of articles published throughout the world.

Kalvelage, Carl, and Morley Segal. *Research Guide in Political Science*. 2nd ed. Morristown, NJ: General Learning Press, 1976. Chapters on researching a topic in political science and writing the paper, basic references, newspapers and columnists, statistics, journals of interest in research, etc.

Parliaments of the World. 2nd ed. Prepared by the Inter-Parliamentary Union. Aldershot, England: Gower, 1986. 2 vols. Comparisons, in parallel columns, of types of electoral systems, nominating methods, ministerial responsibilities, introduction of bills, etc.

Raymond, Walter J. *Dictionary of Politics: Selected American and Foreign Political and Legal Terms*. 6th ed. Lawrenceville, Va.: Brunswick, 1978. Over 4,600 definitions of words and phrases, each definition followed by suggestions for further reading. Numerous appendixes include lists of American presidents and vice-presidents, the Constitution of the United States, the Charter of the United Nations, etc.

Safire, William. *Safire's Political Dictionary: An Enlarged, Up-to-Date Edition of* The New Language of Politics. New York: Random House, 1978. Definitions and extended discussions of some 1,200 words and phrases used in the political world (especially in the US).

Taylor, Charles Lewis, and David A. Jodice. *World Handbook of Political and Social Indicators*. 3rd ed. New Haven: Yale University Press, 1983. 2 vols. Statistical data for over 150 nation-states on such matters as government and military expenditures, distribution of income, newspaper circulation, growth rates, gross national products, etc.

Winter, Herbert R., and Thomas J. Bellows. *People and Politics: An Introduction to Political Science*. 3rd ed. New York: John Wiley and Sons, 1985. A text for beginning students, it surveys the major areas, political analysis, political processes, and international politics.

PSYCHOLOGY

Chun, Ki-Taek, et al. *Measures for Psychological Assessment: A Guide to 3,000 Original Sources and Their Applications*. Ann Arbor, Mich.: Survey Research Center, Institute for Social Research, 1975. List of 3,000 references to publications in which measures were first described, and a list of over 6,000 instances in which these measures were used.

Corsini, Raymond J., ed. *Encyclopedia of Psychology*. New York: John Wiley and Sons, 1984. 4 vols. Over 2,000 entries on subjects and persons (living and dead). Vol. 4 includes subject and name indexes to the first three volumes, and an extensive bibliography.

Dörken, Herbert, et al. *The Professional Psychologist Today*. San Francisco: Jossey-Bass, 1976. Chapters on standards for psychologists, social security programs, mental health services, costs of mental health services, issues facing professional psychologists, etc.

Encyclopedia of Psychology. H.J. Eysenck et al., eds. 3 vols. New York: Herder and Herder, 1972. Brief definitions as well as long articles on important terms and concepts. Numerous bibliographies.

Gregory, Richard L., ed. *The Oxford Companion to the Mind*. Oxford: Oxford University Press, 1987. Over 200 authors have contributed thousands of entries on almost anything having to do with the mind, including computer chess, images of the brain in action, intentionality, perception, infancy, etc. Exhaustive index.

International Encyclopedia of the Social Sciences. David L. Sills, ed. New York: The Free Press; London: Collier Macmillan, 1968. 17 vols. A standard work, with vol. 17 the index to the whole. Vol. 18 (1979) contains 215 biographies, with reading lists, of important scientists.

Popplestone, John A., and Marion White McPherson. *Dictionary of Concepts in General Psychology*. New York: Greenwood, 1988. Detailed discussions of major concepts, each followed by a list of references.

Psychological Abstracts: Nonevaluative Summaries of the Serial Literature in Psychology and Related Disciplines. Arlington, Va.: American Psychological Association. Published yearly since 1927. Volume 75 (for 1988) contains abstracts of over 37,000 articles appearing in journals throughout the world. The key source.

Sales, Bruce Dennis, ed. *The Professional Psychologist's Handbook*. New York: Plenum Press, 1983. Detailed articles on professional standards, professional organizations, relevant laws, managerial skills, professional decision-making, etc.

Wilkening, Howard E. *The Psychology Almanac*. Monterey, Cal.: Brooks/Cole, 1973. Includes, in addition to a dictionary of psychological terms, sections on ethical standards, brief descriptions of 200 journals, explanations of Latin terms used in psychology, and numerous statistical tables.

Wolman, Benjamin B., ed. *Dictionary of Behavioral Science*. 2nd ed. San Diego, Cal.: Academic Press, 1989. Brief definitions covering all areas of psychology, including aspects of applied psychology. Also includes psychiatry, biochemistry, psychopharmacology, and clinical practice.

RELIGIOUS STUDIES

Achtemeier, Paul J., gen. ed. *Harper's Bible Dictionary*. San Francisco: Harper and Row, 1985. Hundreds of articles by some 180 scholars on the Bible and the world from which it came. Includes maps and numerous illustrations.

Barrett, David B., ed. *World Christian Encyclopedia: A Comparative Study of Churches and Religions in the Modern World, AD 1900-2000*. Oxford: Oxford University Press, 1982. Numerous tables, maps, and statistics of Christianity throughout the world, as well as a dictionary of world Christianity in 223 countries, human environment and activity in each section of the world, etc.

Brauer, Jerald C., ed. *The Westminster Dictionary of Church History*. Philadelphia: Westminster Press, 1971. Brief entries on the major people, movements, facts, and events of Christianity, from earliest times to the 1960s.

Eliade, Mircea, ed. in chief. *The Encyclopedia of Religion*. New York: Macmillan, 1987. 16 vols. Thousands of descriptive and interpretive essays on all aspects of religion, from earliest times to the present. Numerous bibliographies. Vol. 16 is the index to the whole work.

Gorman, G.E., and Lyn Gorman. *Theological and Religious Reference Materials*. New York: Greenwood Press, 1984-86. 3 vols. An annotated bibliography of general reference works, biblical studies, church history, religious orders, theology, liturgy, music, counselling, etc.

Hinnells, John R., ed. *A Handbook of Living Religions*. New York: Viking, 1984. Detailed articles on Judaism, Christianity, Islam, Hinduism, Buddhism, and other major religions. Includes diagrams, charts, and bibliographies.

————, ed. *The Penguin Dictionary of Religions*. London: Allen Lane, 1984. Over 1,100 entries on the world's major and minor religions. Extensive bibliography and index.

Kepple, Robert J. *Reference Works for Theological Research: An Annotated Selective Bibliographical Guide*. 2nd ed. Washington, DC: University

Press of America, 1981. Chapters on religious-theological encycloedias and handbooks, biographical sources, book review and periodical indexes, biblical studies, church history, church music, etc.

Wilson, John F., and Thomas P. Slavens. *Research Guide to Religious Studies*. Chicago: American Library Association, 1982. Part I deals with the study and history of religions, religious thought and ethics, the scientific study of religion, etc. Part II is an extensive, annotated list of reference works: atlases, bibliographies, dictionaries, handbooks, etc., with, in the last section, books that deal with particular religions.

SOCIOLOGY

Aby, Stephen H. *Sociology: A Guide to Reference and Information Sources*. Littleton, Col.: Libraries Unlimited, Inc., 1987. Descriptions of over 600 of the major reference works in sociology and related social sciences. Index by author, title, and subject.

Annual Review of Sociology, vol. 13, 1987. W. Richard Scott, ed. Palo Alto, Calif.: Annual Reviews Inc., 1987. Survey essays on ''recent important sociological theory and research in specialized fields''.

Bart, Pauline, and Linda Frankel. *The Student Sociologist's Handbook*. 4th ed. New York: Random House, 1986. Includes an overview of sociology, and chapters on writing a sociology paper, doing research, periodical literature, guides to research, etc.

Cumulative Index of Sociology Journals, 1971-1985. Judith C. Lantz, comp. Washington: American Sociological Association, 1987. Listings, by author and subject, of all articles published from 1971 to 1985 in ten of the key journals.

International Bibliography of the Social Sciences, 1985. London and New York: Routledge, 1988. Prepared by the International Committee for Social Science Information and Documentation. Published regularly since 1952, this bibliography lists books, articles, and pamphlets from much of the world, in a variety of languages.

International Encyclopedia of the Social Sciences. David L. Sills, ed. New York: The Free Press, London: Collier Macmillan, 1968. 17 vols. A standard work, with vol. 17 the index to the whole. Vol. 18 (1979) contains 215 biographies, with reading lists, of important scientists.

Li, Tze-chung. *Social Science Reference Sources: A Practical Guide*. West-port, Conn.: Greenwood Press, 1980. Includes chapters on statistical sources, government publications, data archives, and subdisciplines of the social sciences, such as cultural anthropology, economics, law, political science, etc.

A New Dictionary of Sociology. G. Duncan Mitchell, ed. London: Rout-ledge and Kegan Paul, 1979. Definitions and explanations of the most important sociological terms, some in considerable detail. Also includes sociologists.

Social Sciences Index. Joseph Bloomfield, ed. New York: H.H. Wilson. Published from 1907 to 1965 as the *International Index*, from 1965 to 1974 as the *Social Sciences and Humanities Index*, and since 1974 under its present title. Extensive listing of the major sociology journals in English and articles published during the year. Numerous sub-head-ings. A key reference.

Webb, William H., et al. *Sources of Information in the Social Sciences: A Guide to the Literature*. 3rd ed. Chicago: American Library Association, 1986. Includes chapters on Sociology, Anthropology, and Psychol-ogy. Each discipline is dealt with in a "Survey of the Field" and a "Survey of the Reference Works". Includes bibliographies for each field.

VISUAL ARTS

Christensen, Erwin O. *A Guide to Art Museums in the United States*. New York: Dodd, Mead, 1968. Descriptions of the major holdings of over 80 museums throughout the country.

Ehresmann, Donald L. *Fine Arts: A Bibliographic Guide to Basic Reference Works, Histories, and Handbooks*. Littleton, Col.: Libraries Unlimited, 1979. An annotated bibliography of bibliographies, dictionaries, encyclopedias, histories, and handbooks. Excellent author-title-sub-ject index.

Ekdahl, Janis. *American Sculpture: A Guide to Information Sources*. Detroit: Gale, 1977. An annotated bibliography of American sculp-ture over the past 250 years, including such matters as bibliographies, sources of biographical information, surveys of American sculpture, individual sculptors, etc.

Encyclopedia of World Art. New York: McGraw-Hill, 1959-1967. 16 vols. An exhaustive and scholarly discussion of all the arts throughout the world, from earliest times to the present.

Jones, Lois Swan. *Art Research Methods and Resources: A Guide to Finding Art Information*. Dubuque, Iowa: Kendall/Hunt, 1978. Chapters on conducting research, understanding art museum catalogues, researching an author's credentials, catalogues of holdings of famous libraries, book review sources, etc.

MacDonald, Colin S., comp. *A Dictionary of Canadian Artists*. Ottawa: Canadian Paperbacks Publishing, 1975-1982. Detailed biographies of Canadian painters, sculptors, engravers, and potters, both living and dead. Bibliography following each entry. Volume 6, the most recent, ends with Rakine.

Myers, Bernard S., ed. *McGraw-Hill Dictionary of Art*. New York: McGraw-Hill, 1969. 5 vols. Over 15,000 entries, by 125 contributors, including artists' biographies and articles on styles, periods, cities, buildings, museums, and definitions.

Osborne, Harold, ed. *The Oxford Companion to Art*. Oxford: Clarendon, 1970. Detailed entries, arranged alphabetically, on all the visual arts, but excluding theatre, film, and dance. The world-wide scope takes in all time.

Read, Herbert, consulting ed. *Encyclopaedia of the Arts*. New York: Meredith Press, 1966. Over 10,000 entries on individual artists and works of art, historical movements, techniques, and materials. Profusely illustrated.

Richards, J.M., ed. *Who's Who in Architecture: From 1400 to the Present*. New York: Holt, Rinehart and Winston, 1977. Articles, arranged alphabetically, on over 600 architects and designers, from about 1400 to the present, from around the world. Illustrations, and index, by country, of all the buildings dealt with in the text.

Simard, Cyril. *Artisanat Québécois*. Montréal: Editions de l'homme, 1975-1977. 3 vols. Deals with wood carving, textiles, pottery, glasswork, bookbinding, and Indian and Eskimo art. Many illustrations. In French.

Sokol, David M. *American Architecture and Art: A Guide to Information Sources*. Detroit: Gale, 1976. An annotated bibliography of over 1,500 sources concerning American painting, architecture, sculpture, furniture, ceramics, and textiles.

6
CRITICAL
approaches

The student who has spent some time reading literature and who has been involved, even if only briefly, with literary criticism, knows that there are a number of ways of approaching a novel, a poem, or an essay. With regard to the same novel, for instance, one can take the following approaches: the pragmatic (how useful is this novel in teaching moral values?), the mimetic (how well does this book represent reality?), the biographical (to what extent does this novel reveal the author's own life?), the historical (how accurately does this book represent the world during the time it was written?), the Marxist (to what extent does this book represent the struggle of the working class against the proletariat?), the feminist (does this novel accurately depict the status of women?). And so on—there are still other possible approaches.

The same types of critical approaches can also be used with regard to other branches of the humanities. For instance, a film can be examined pragmatically, or biographically, or historically, or from the Marxist or feminist points of view. This is not to say, however, that all critical approaches can be applied to all disciplines in the humanities; it might, for example, be difficult to apply the mimetic approach to the study of economics. However, most of the critical approaches discussed in this chapter can be applied to most areas of the humanities.

This chapter offers brief explanations of some of the most important kinds of criticism. Students who are majoring in psychology or history or art criticism or American literature will find that some of these approaches are already familiar; they will find, in addition, that some of the approaches that are new to them can also be applied to the discipline they are studying. (Exception is made here of a few types of contemporary criticism, such as structuralism, post-structuralism, and semiotics, which are too complex and difficult to be dealt with here, and are not often discussed in undergraduate courses).

As you study these critical approaches, and later try to apply them to various topics in sociology, or history, or anthropology, you must remember that criticism is not a precise science; in the humanities there is room not only for a wide variety of ways of approaching the same text, but for considerable differences within each single approach. And this is one of the most satisfying aspects of applying a critical method to an interesting text.

Archetypal. Archetypal criticism (the word means a prototype, or a pattern from which copies are made) reveals the basic patterns of a culture, patterns that have timeless, universal appeal. These patterns usually take the form of myths — that is, stories about the exploits of gods or goddesses or extraordinary humans — that have their origins in the Bible, in ancient Greek and Roman literature, in Norse and Anglo-Saxon sagas, etc. Some of the most common myths have to do with such topics as death and rebirth, the earth mother, the search for the father, the enchanted prince, the divine child, the journey underground, etc.

Biographical. The biographical critic investigates the life of the writer in order to use knowledge of the life to clarify the work. Such knowledge can help to explain, in the written work, the stand an author takes on a particular problem. It can also intensify the effect of a work by revealing the circumstances in which the author worked while writing the book: the influences and pressures under which she worked, for instance, or the people she knew closely, or the books she read at the time she was writing, or the physical and emotional difficulties she had to work under, etc.

Feminism. Feminist criticism has a number of objectives. It seeks to counter sexist attitudes of the past (and present) according to which both the nature of women and their role in society were secondary to those of men; it attempts to evaluate the exact role of women in cultural history; it fights the stereotypes of women in literature; it argues that any criticism of society must include the feminine consciousness — and, in short, it tries to reshape any system of values in which the role of women has been slighted.

Freudian. Freudian criticism (which is closely allied to psychological criticism) emphasizes the unconscious aspects of the human mind, from which springs the creative impulse. By means of his numerous case studies in psychoanalysis, Freud was able to show that the impulse to create comes from the *id* (which is in the unconscious mind and is associated with instincts and primitive needs), the *ego* (the conscious mediator of the *id*'s requirements), and the *superego* (the conscience, which develops as the result of the community's moral standards). In short, he revealed that much of the activity of the human mind lies in the unconscious, a revelation that has had a profound effect on modern culture.

Historical. For the historical critic, what is important in dealing with a book is the historical context when it was written. That is, the book was written in a specific place, in a specific social context, and at a specific time, and in order to understand the book thoroughly we need to understand it within these boundaries. The book is, in other words, the product of such factors as race, time, and nationality; and in order to fully comprehend the book we must know and understand these factors.

Impressionism. At its crudest, impressionistic criticism takes a form along the lines of ''I may not know much about this subject, but I know what I like and I like this.'' This kind of criticism — the response, or impression, that the work makes on the reader or viewer — has long been used to comment on almost any subject. The danger of impressionistic criticism is that it can be based largely on ignorance. At its best, however — when it is based on discriminating taste and thorough knowledge of the subject — this approach can be perceptive, valuable, and enjoyable.

Marxism. Marxist criticism stands apart from all other types of criticism in that it is the only one that has a political aim. The Marxist critic, that is, recognizes that the author's work has been profoundly influenced by economic and social forces, and recognizes also that knowledge of these forces will contribute to the transformation of the world. It is this transformation, either by evolution or by revolution, that is at the centre of Marxism. Thus the Marxist studies everything as part of a larger project, a political one, that has as its principal aim the changing of society, particularly of the lower social class, the workers.

Mimesis. Although the term *mimesis* is difficult to pin down precisely, it can generally be said that a mimetic approach is one that is concerned with the relationship between the work and the world that the work is intended to reproduce. Thus the principal criterion of the mimetic approach is the extent to which the work is truthful to the reality it tries to represent. The reader is thus concerned with the realism of the work.

New Criticism. The New Criticism (so-called because it was a reaction against older kinds of criticism, especially the historical and the biographical) insists on a close reading of the book, without reference to any sort of biographical or social background. The New Critic emphasizes that everything necessary for an analysis of a book is already present in the book itself; all other matters — such as the author's life, or the historical, social, and economic background — are irrelevant. The reader must concentrate on the work itself and evaluate it in terms of its own structure and values.

Pragmatism. The pragmatic approach is concerned with the effect of a work on its audience — the moral lessons it teaches, or the pleasure it gives, or the good it produces. Thus the value of a work is related to its usefulness, its utility. This sort of criticism is also often referred to as practical criticism, or applied criticism, and is thus distinguished from the purely theoretical. Practical criticism judges the value of a work by the degree of success the work achieves in affecting its audience.

Psychological. For many writers today, there is little difference between psychological criticism and Freudian criticism. Nevertheless, it can be usefully said that psychological criticism is the application of the principles of modern psychology either to characters or situations in a work, to the writer of the work, or to the effects of the work on its readers. Thus psychological criticism is clearly the basis of other kinds of criticism, particularly impressionistic and biographical criticism. Since, as Freud demonstrated, there is a creative process in every human, we must look at the psychic make-up of the individual in order to determine the nature of the personality.

7
WRITING
examinations

Most students feel nervous before tests and exams. It's not surprising. Writing an essay exam — even the open-book or take-home kind — imposes special pressures because both the time and the questions are restricted: you can't write and rewrite the way you can in a regular essay, and you must often write on topics you would otherwise choose to avoid. And although on the surface objective tests may look easier, because you don't have to compose the answers, they force you to be more decisive about your answers than essay exams do. You know that to do your best you need to feel calm — but how? These general guidelines will help you approach any test or exam with confidence. For special advice on open-book and take-home exams, see pp. 72 – 3; for objective tests, see p. 73.

Before the exam

Review regularly

A weekly review of lecture notes and texts will help you not only to remember important material but to relate new information to old. If you don't review regularly, at the end of the year you'll be faced with relearning rather than remembering.

Set memory triggers

As you review, condense and focus the material by writing down in the margin key words or phrases that will trigger off a whole set of details in your mind. The trigger might be a concept word that names or points to an important theory or definition, or a quantitative phrase such as "three causes of the decline in manufacturing" or "five reasons for inflation."

Sometimes you can create an acronym or a nonsense sentence that will trigger an otherwise hard-to-remember set of facts—something like the acronym HOMES (Huron, Ontario, Michigan, Erie, Superior) for the Great Lakes. Since the difficulty of memorizing increases with the number of individual items you are trying to remember, any method that will reduce that number will increase your effectiveness.

Ask questions: try the three-C approach

Think of questions that will get to the heart of the material and cause you to examine the relations between various subjects or issues; then figure out how you would answer them. The three-C approach discussed on p. 7 may be a help. For example, reviewing the *components* of the subject could mean focusing on the main parts of an issue or on the definitions of major terms or theories. When reviewing *change* in the subject, you might ask yourself what elements caused it, directly or indirectly. To review *context* you might consider how certain aspects of the subject—issues, theories, actions, results—compare with others on the course. Essentially, what the three-C approach does is force you to look at the material from various perspectives.

Old examinations are useful both for seeing the type of question you might be asked and for checking on the thoroughness of your preparation. If old exams aren't available, you might get together with friends who are taking the same course and ask each other questions. Just remember that the most useful review questions are not the ones that require you to recall facts, but those that force you to analyse, integrate, or evaluate information.

Allow extra time

Give yourself lots of time to get to the exam. Nothing is more nerve-wracking than to think that you're going to be late. If you have to travel, don't forget that traffic can jam, and so can alarm clocks—remember Murphy's Law: "Whatever can go wrong will." Anticipate any unusual difficulties and allow yourself a good margin.

Writing an essay exam
Read the exam

An exam is not a hundred-metre dash; instead of starting to write immediately, take time at the beginning to read through each question and create a plan of action. A few minutes spent on thinking and organizing will bring better results than the same time spent on writing a few more lines.

Apportion your time

Reread the instructions carefully to find out how many questions you must answer and to see if you have any choice. Subtract five minutes or so for the initial planning, then divide the time you have left by the number of questions you have to answer. If possible, allow for a little extra time at the end to reread and edit your work. If the instructions on the exam indicate that not all questions are of equal value, apportion your time accordingly.

Choose your questions

Decide on the questions that you will do and the order in which you will do them. Your answers don't have to be in the same order as the questions. If you think you have lots of time, it's a good idea to place your best answer first, your worst answers in the middle, and your second best answer at the end, in order to leave the reader on a high note. If you think you will be rushed, though, it's wiser to work from best to worst. That way you will be sure to get all the marks you can on your good answers, and you won't have to cut a good answer short at the end.

Keep calm

If your first reaction on reading the exam is "I can't do any of it!" force yourself to keep calm; take ten slow, deep breaths as a deliberate relaxation exercise. Decide which is the question that you can answer best. Even if the exam seems disastrous at first, you can probably find one question that looks manageable: that's the one to begin with. It will get you rolling and increase your confidence. By the time you have finished, you are likely to find that your mind has worked through to the answer for another question.

Read each question carefully

As you turn to each question, read it again carefully and underline all the key words. The wording will probably suggest the number of parts your answer should have; be sure you don't overlook anything (a common mistake when people are nervous). Since the verb used in the question is usually a guide for the approach to take in your answer, it's especially important that you interpret the following terms correctly:

- *explain*: show the how's or why's;
- *compare*: give both similarities and differences—even if the question doesn't say *compare and contrast*;
- *outline*: state simply, without much development of each point (unless specifically asked);
- *discuss*: develop your points in an orderly way, taking into account contrary evidence or ideas.

Make notes

Before you even begin to organize your answer, jot down key ideas and information related to the topic on rough paper or the unlined pages of your answer book. These notes will save you the worry of forgetting something by the time you begin writing. Next, arrange those parts you want to use into a brief plan.

Be direct

Get to the points quickly and illustrate them frequently. In an exam, as opposed to a term paper, it's best to use a direct approach. Don't worry about composing a graceful introduction: simply state the main points that you are going to discuss, then get on with developing them. Remember that your paper will likely be one of many read and marked by someone who has to work quickly—the clearer your answers are, the better they will be received.

For each main point give the kind of specific details that will prove you really know the material. General statements will show you are able to assimilate information, but they need examples to back them up.

Write legibly

Writing that's hard to read produces a cranky reader. When the marker has to struggle to decipher your ideas, you may get poorer results than you deserve. If for some special reason (such as a physical handicap) your writing is hard to read, see if you can make special arrangements to use a typewriter. If your writing is just plain bad, it's probably better to print.

Write on alternate lines

Writing on every other line will not only make your writing easier to read, but leave you space for changes and additions; you won't have to cover your paper with a lot of messy circles and arrows.

Keep to your time plan

Keep to your plan and don't skip any questions. Try to write something on each topic. Remember that it's easier to score half marks for a question you don't know much about than it is to score full marks for one you could write pages on. If you find yourself running out of time on an answer and still haven't finished, summarize the remaining points and go on to the next question. Leave a large space between questions so that you can go back and add more if you have time. If you write a new ending, remember to cross out the old one—neatly.

Reread your answers

No matter how tired or fed up you are, reread your answers at the end, if there's time. Check especially for clarity of expression; try to get rid of confusing sentences and increase the logical connection between your ideas. Revisions that make answers easier to read are always worth the effort.

Writing an open-book exam

If you think that permission to take your books into the exam room is an "Open Sesame" to success, be forewarned. You could fall into the trap of relying too heavily on them; you may spend so much time rifling through pages and looking things up that you won't have time to write good answers. The result may be worse than if you had been allowed no books at all.

If you want to do well, use your books only to check information and look up specific, hard-to-remember details for a topic you already know a good deal about. For instance, if your subject is history you can look up exact dates or quotations; for a business subject you can look up voting statistics; for an exam in social theory you can check some classical references and find the authors' exact definitions of key concepts—if you know where to find them quickly. In other words, use the books to make sure your answers are precise and well illustrated. Never use them to replace studying and careful exam preparation.

Writing a take-home exam

The benefit of a take-home exam is that you have time to plan your answers and to consult your texts or other sources. The catch is that the time is usually less than it would be for an ordinary essay. Don't work yourself into a frenzy trying to respond with a polished research essay for each question; rather, use the extra time to create a well-written exam answer. Keep in mind that you were given this assign-ment to test your overall command of the course: your reader is likely to be less concerned with your specialized research than with evidence that you have understood and assimilated the material.

The guidelines for a take-home exam are therefore similar to those for a regular exam; the only difference is that you don't need to keep such a close eye on the clock:

1. Keep your introduction short and get to the point quickly.
2. Have a straightforward and obvious organizational pattern so that the reader can easily see your main ideas.
3. Use frequent concrete examples to back up your points.
4. Where possible, show the range of your knowledge of course material by referring to a number of different sources, rather than constantly using the same ones.
5. Try to show that you can analyse and evaluate material: that you can do more than simply repeat information.

Writing an objective test

Objective tests are common in the social sciences. Although some-times the questions are the true-false kind, most often they are multiple-choice. The main difficulty with these tests is that their questions are designed to confuse the student who is not certain of the correct answers. If you are one of those people who are forever second-guessing themselves, or who readily see two sides to every question, you may find objective tests particularly hard at first. Fortunately, practice almost always improves performance.

Preparation for objective tests is the same as for other kinds. Here, though, it's especially important to pay attention to definitions and unexpected or confusing pieces of information, because they can so readily be adapted to make objective-test questions. Although there is no sure recipe for doing well on an objective test — other than knowing the course material completely and confidently — these suggestions may help you to do better:

Find out the marking system

If marks are based solely on the number of right answers, you should pick an answer for every question even if you aren't sure it's the right one. For a true-false question you have a 50-per-cent chance that it will be; and even for a multiple-choice question with four possible answers, you would get an average of 25 per cent right if you picked the answers blindfolded.

On the other hand, if there is a penalty for wrong answers—if marks are deducted for errors—you should guess only when you are fairly sure you are right, or when you are able to rule out most of the possibilities. Don't make wild guesses.

Do the easy questions first

Go through the test at least twice. On the first round, don't waste time on troublesome questions. Since the questions are usually of equal value, it's best to get all the marks you can on the ones you find easy. You can tackle the more difficult questions on the next round. This approach has two advantages:

1. You won't be forced, because you have run out of time, to leave out any questions that you could easily have answered correctly.
2. When you come back to a difficult question on the second round, you may find that in the meantime you have figured out the answer.

Make your guesses educated ones

If you have decided to guess, at least increase your chance of getting the answers right. Forget about intuition, hunches, and lucky numbers. More important, forget about so-called patterns of correct answers—the idea that if there have been two "A" answers in a row, the next one can't possibly be "A", or that if there hasn't been a "true" for a while, "true" must be a good guess. Unfortunately, many test-setters either don't worry about patterns at all, or else deliberately elude pattern-hunters by giving the right answer the same letter or number several times in a row.

Remember that constructing good objective tests is a special skill that not all instructors have mastered. Often the questions they pose, though sound enough as questions, do not produce enough realistic alternatives for answers. In such cases the test-setter may resort to some less-realistic options, and if you keep your eyes open you can spot them. James F. Shepherd[1] has suggested a number of tips that will increase your chances of making the right guess:

- Start by weeding out all the answers you know are wrong, rather than looking for the right one.
- Avoid any terms you don't recognize. Some students are taken in by anything that looks like sophisticated terminology and may

assume that such answers must be correct. They are usually wrong: the unfamiliar term may well be a red herring, especially if it is close in sound to the correct one.

- Avoid extremes. Most often the right answer lies in between. For example, suppose that the options are the numbers 800,000; 350,000; 275,000; and 15: the highest and lowest numbers are likely to be wrong.
- Avoid absolutes, especially on questions dealing with people. Few aspects of human life are as certain as is implied by such words as *everyone, all,* or *no one; always, invariably,* or *never.* Statements containing these words are usually false.
- Avoid jokes or humorous statements.
- Avoid demeaning or insulting statements. Like jokes, these are usually inserted simply to provide a full complement of options.
- Choose the best available answer, even if it is not indisputably true.
- Choose the long answer over the short (it's more likely to contain the detail needed to make it right) and the particular statement over the general (generalizations are usually too sweeping to be true).
- Choose "all of the above" over individual answers. Test-setters know that students with a patchy knowledge of the course material will often fasten on the one fact they know. Only those with a thorough knowledge will recognize that all the answers listed are correct.

Two final tips

If you have time at the end of the exam, go back and reread the questions. One or two wrong answers caused by misreading can make a significant difference to your score. On the other hand, don't start second-guessing yourself and changing a lot of answers at the last minute. Studies have shown that when students make changes they are often wrong. Stick to your decisions unless you know for certain you have made a mistake.

NOTES
[1]James F. Shepherd, *College Study Skills* (Boston: Houghton Mifflin, 1979) and *RSVP: The Houghton Mifflin Reading, Study, and Vocabulary Program* (Boston: Houghton Mifflin. 1981).

8
WRITING
with style

Writing with style does not mean stuffing your prose with fancy words and extravagant images. Any style, from the simplest to the most elaborate, can be effective depending on the occasion and intent. Writers known for their style are those who have projected something of their own personality into their writing; we can hear a distinctive voice in what they say. Obviously it takes time to develop a unique style. To begin, you have to decide what general effect you want to create.

Taste in style reflects the times. In earlier centuries, when few people outside the leisured class ever had a chance to read, many respected writers wrote in an elaborate style that we would think much too wordy. Now almost all of us read, but newspapers, television, and radio compete with books for our attention, and as a result we tend to favour a simpler kind of writing. Journalists have led the trend towards short, easy-to-grasp sentences and paragraphs. Writing in an academic context, you may expect your audience to be more reflective than the average newspaper reader, but the most effective style is still one that is clear, concise, and forceful.

BE CLEAR

Since sentence structure is dealt with in Chapter 9, this section will focus on clear wording and paragraphing.

Choose clear words

A good dictionary is a wise investment; get into the habit of using one. It will give you not only common meanings, but less familiar applications, archaic uses, and derivations, as well as proper spelling.

Canadian usage and spelling may follow either British or American practices, but usually combine aspects of both; you should check before you buy a dictionary to be sure that it gives these variants.

A thesaurus lists words that are closely related in meaning. It can help when you want to avoid repeating yourself, or when you are fumbling for a word that's on the tip of your tongue. But be careful: make sure you remember the difference between denotative and connotative meanings. A word's denotation is its primary or "dictionary" meaning. Its connotations are any associations that it may suggest; they may not be as exact as the denotations, but they are part of the impression the word conveys. If you examine a list of "synonyms" in a thesaurus, you will see that even words with similar meanings can have dramatically different connotations. For example, alongside the word *indifferent* your thesaurus may give the following: *neutral*, *unconcerned*, *careless*, *easy-going*, *unambitious*, and *half-hearted*. Imagine the different impressions you would create if you chose one or the other of those words to complete this sentence: "Questioned about the experiment's chance of success, he was _____ in his response." In order to write clearly, you must remember that a reader may react to the suggestive meaning of a word as much as to its "dictionary" meaning.

Use plain English

Plain words are almost always more forceful than fancy ones. If you aren't sure what plain English is, think of everyday speech: how do you talk to your friends? Many of our most common words—the ones that sound most natural and direct—are short. A good number of them are also among the oldest words in the English language. By contrast, most of the words that English has derived from other languages are longer and more complicated; even after they've been used for centuries, they can still sound artificial. For this reason you should beware of words loaded with prefixes (*pre-*, *post-*, *anti-*, *pro-*, *sub-*, *maxi-*, etc.) and suffixes (*-ate*, *-ize*, *-tion*, etc.). These Latinate attachments can make individual words more precise and efficient, but putting a lot of them together will make your writing seem dense and hard to understand. In many cases you can substitute a plain word for a fancy one:

Fancy	*Plain*
determinant	cause
utilization	use

cognizant	aware
obviate	prevent
terminate	end
infuriate	anger
oration	speech
conclusion	end
requisite	needed
numerous	many
finalize	finish, complete
systematize	order
sanitize	clean
remuneration	pay
maximization	increase

Suggesting that you write in plain English does not mean that you should never pick an unfamiliar, long, or foreign word: sometimes those words are the only ones that will convey precisely what you mean. Inserting an unusual expression into a passage of plain writing can also be an effective means of catching the reader's attention—as long as you don't do it too often.

Be precise

Always be as precise or exact as you can. Avoid all-purpose adjectives like *major*, *significant*, and *important*, and vague verbs such as *involve*, *entail*, and *exist*, when you can be more specific:

orig · Donald Smith <u>was involved in</u> the construction of the CPR.

rev. Donald Smith <u>helped finance</u> the construction of the CPR.

Here's another example:

orig · Granting public-service employees the right to strike was a <u>significant</u> legacy of Lester Pearson's years as Prime Minister.

rev. Granting public-service employees the right to strike was a <u>costly</u> legacy of Lester Pearson's years as Prime Minister.

(or)

rev. Granting public-service employees the right to strike was a <u>beneficial</u> legacy of Lester Pearson's years as Prime Minister.

Avoid unnecessary qualifiers

Qualifiers such as *very*, *rather*, and *extremely* are over-used. Experienced writers know that saying something is *very beautiful* may have less impact than saying simply that it is *beautiful*. For example, compare these sentences:

> That is a beautiful garden.
>
> That is a very beautiful garden.

Which has more punch?

When you think that an adjective needs qualifying—and sometimes it will—first see if it's possible to change either the adjective or the phrasing. Instead of writing

> Imperial Castings made a very big profit last year.

write

> Imperial Castings made an unprecedented profit last year.

or (if you aren't sure whether or not the profit actually set a record):

> Imperial Castings' profit rose forty per cent last year.

In some cases qualifiers not only weaken your writing but are redundant, since the adjectives themselves are absolutes. To say that something is *very unique* makes as much—or as little—sense as to say that someone is *rather pregnant* or *very dead*.

Avoid fancy jargon

All academic subjects have their own terminology; it may be unfamiliar to outsiders but it helps specialists to explain things to each other. The trouble is that people sometimes use jargon—special, technical language—unnecessarily, thinking it will make them seem more knowledgeable. Too often the result is not clarity, but complication. The guideline is easy: use specialized terminology only when it's a kind of shorthand that will help you explain something more precisely and efficiently. If plain prose will do just as well, stick to it.

Creating clear paragraphs

Paragraphs come in so many sizes and patterns that no single formula could possibly cover them all. The two basic principles to remember are these: (1) a paragraph is a means of developing and framing an idea or impression, and (2) the divisions between paragraphs aren't random, but indicate a shift in focus.

Develop your ideas

You are not likely to sit down and consciously ask yourself "What pattern shall I use to develop this paragraph? What comes first is the idea you intend to develop: the pattern the paragraph takes should flow from the idea itself and the way you want to discuss or expand it. (The most common ways of developing an idea are outlined on pp. 15–17.)

You may take one or several paragraphs to develop an idea fully. For a definition alone you could write one paragraph or ten, depending on the complexity of the subject and the nature of the assignment. Just remember that ideas need development, and that each new paragraph signals a change in idea.

Consider the topic sentence

Skilled skim-readers know that they can get the general drift of a book simply by reading the first sentence of each paragraph. The reason is that most paragraphs begin by stating the central idea to be developed. If you are writing your essay from a formal plan, you will probably find that each section and subsection will generate the topic sentence for a new paragraph.

Like the thesis statement for the essay as a whole, the topic sentence is not obligatory: in some paragraphs the controlling idea is not stated until the middle or even the end, and in others it is not stated at all but merely implied. Nevertheless, it's a good idea to think out a topic sentence for every paragraph. That way you'll be sure that each one has a readily graspable point and is clearly connected to what comes before and after. When revising your initial draft, check to see that each paragraph is held together by a topic sentence, either stated or implied. If you find that you can't formulate one, you should probably rework the whole paragraph.

Maintain focus

To be clear a paragraph should contain only those details that are in some way related to the central idea. It must also be structured so that the details are easily *seen* to be related. One way of showing these relations is to keep the same grammatical subject in most of the sentences that make up the paragraph. When the grammatical subject is shifting all the time, a paragraph loses focus, as in the following example:[1]

orig · Boys in school play a variety of sports these days. In the fall, football still attracts the most, although an increasing number now play soccer. For some basketball is the favourite when the ball season is over, but you will find that swimming or gymnastics are also popular. Cold winter temperatures may allow the school to have an outdoor rink, and then hockey becomes a source of enjoyment for many. In spring, though, the rinks begin melting, and so there is less opportunity to play. Then some boys take up soccer again, while track and field also attracts many participants.

Here the grammatical subject (underlined) is constantly jumping from one thing to another. Notice how much stronger the focus becomes when all the sentences have the same grammatical subject—either the same noun, a synonym, or a related pronoun:

new · Boys in school play a variety of sports these days. In the fall, most still choose football, although an increasing number now play soccer. When the ball season is over, some turn to basketball; others prefer swimming or gymnastics. If cold winter temperatures permit an outdoor rink, many boys enjoy hockey. Once the ice begins to melt in spring, though, they can play less often. Then some take up soccer again, while others choose track and field.

Naturally it's not always possible to retain the same grammatical subject throughout a paragraph. If you were comparing the athletic pursuits of boys and girls, for example, you would have to switch back and forth between boys and girls as your grammatical subject. In the same way, you will have to shift when you are discussing examples of an idea or exceptions to it.

Avoid monotony

If most or all of the sentences in your paragraph have the same grammatical subject, how do you avoid boring your reader? There are two easy ways:

Use stand-in words. Pronouns, either personal (*I, we, you, he, she, it, they*) or demonstrative (*this, that, those*) can stand in for the subject, as can synonyms (words or phrases that mean the same thing). The revised paragraph on boys' sports, for example, uses the pronouns *some, most,* and *they* as substitutes for *boys*. Most well-written paragraphs have a liberal sprinkling of these stand-in words.

''Bury'' the subject by putting something in front of it. When the subject is placed in the middle of the sentence rather than at the beginning, it's less obvious to the reader. If you take another look at the revised paragraph, you'll see that in several sentences there is a word or phrase in front of the subject, giving the paragraph a feeling of variety. Even a single word, such as *first*, *then*, *lately*, or *moreover*, will do the trick. (Incidentally, this is a useful technique to remember when you are writing a letter of application and want to avoid starting every sentence with *I*.)

Link your ideas

To create coherent paragraphs, you need to link your ideas clearly. Linking words are those connectors—conjunctions and conjunctive adverbs—that show the *relations* between one sentence, or part of a sentence, and another; they're also known as transition words, because they bridge the transition from one thought to another. Make a habit of using linking words when you shift from one grammatical subject or idea to another, whether the shift occurs within a single paragraph or as you move from one paragraph to the next. Here are some of the most common connectors and the logical relations they indicate:

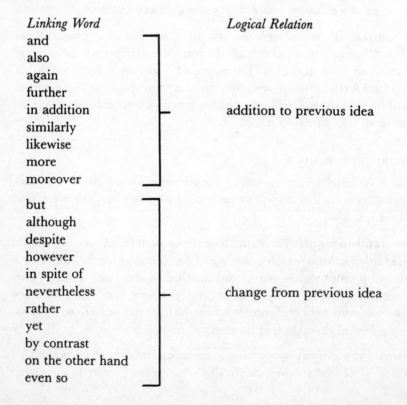

Linking Word	*Logical Relation*
and	
also	
again	
further	
in addition	addition to previous idea
similarly	
likewise	
more	
moreover	
but	
although	
despite	
however	
in spite of	
nevertheless	change from previous idea
rather	
yet	
by contrast	
on the other hand	
even so	

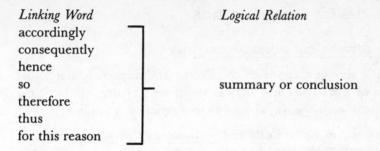

Linking Word	Logical Relation
accordingly	
consequently	
hence	
so	summary or conclusion
therefore	
thus	
for this reason	

Numerical terms such as *first*, *second*, and *third* also work well as links.

Vary the length, but avoid extremes

Ideally, academic writing will have a comfortable balance of long and short paragraphs. Avoid the extremes, especially the one-sentence paragraph, which can only state an idea, without explaining or developing it. A series of very short paragraphs is usually a sign that you have not developed your ideas in enough detail, or that you have started new paragraphs unnecessarily. On the other hand, a succession of long paragraphs can be tiring and difficult to read. In deciding when to start a new paragraph, remember always to consider what is clearest and most helpful for the reader.

BE CONCISE

At one time or another, you will probably be tempted to pad your writing. Whatever the reason—because you need to write two or three thousand words and have only enough to say for one thousand, or just because you think length is strength and hope to get a better mark for the extra—padding is a mistake. You may fool some of the people some of the time, but you are not likely to impress a first-rate mind with second-rate verbiage.

Strong writing is always concise. It leaves out anything that does not serve some communicative or stylistic purpose, in order to say as much as possible in as few words as possible. Concise writing will help you do better on both your essays and your exams.

Guidelines for concise writing

1. Use adverbs and adjectives sparingly

Avoid the shot-gun approach to adverbs and adjectives; don't just spray your work with modifiers in the hope that one will hit. One well-chosen word is always better than a series of synonyms:

orig. As well as being <u>costly</u> and <u>financially extravagant,</u> the venture is <u>reckless</u> and <u>foolhardy.</u>

rev. The venture is <u>foolhardy</u> as well as <u>costly.</u>

2. Avoid noun clusters

A recent trend in some writing is to use nouns as adjectives, as in the phrase *noun cluster*. This device can be effective occasionally, but frequent use can produce a monstrous pile-up of words. Breaking up noun clusters may not always produce fewer words, but it will make your writing easier to read:

orig. word-processor utilization manual
rev. manual for using word-processors

orig. pollution investigation committee
rev. committee to investigate pollution

3. Avoid chains of relative clauses

Sentences full of clauses beginning with *which*, *that*, or *who* are usually more wordy than necessary. Try reducing some of those clauses to phrases or single words:

orig. The solutions <u>which</u> were discussed last night have a practical benefit <u>which</u> is easily grasped by people <u>who</u> have no technical training.

rev. The solutions discussed last night have a practical benefit, easily grasped by non-technical people.

4. Try reducing clauses to phrases or words

Independent clauses can often be reduced by subordination. Here are a few examples:

orig. The report was written in a clear and concise manner and it was widely read.

rev Written in a clear and concise manner, the report was widely read.

rev. Clear and concise, the report was widely read.

orig His plan was of a radical nature and was a source of embarrassment to his employer.

rev. His radical plan embarrassed his employer.

For more detail on subordination and reduction, see p. 84.

5. Strike out hackneyed expressions and circumlocutions

Trite or roundabout phrases may flow from your pen without a thought, but they make for stale prose. Unnecessary words are deadwood; be prepared to hunt and chop ruthlessly to keep your writing vital:

Wordy	Revised
due to the fact that	because
at this point in time	now
consensus of opinion	consensus
in the near future	soon
when all is said and done	(omit)
in the eventuality that	if
in all likelihood	likely

6. Avoid "it is" and "there is" beginnings

Although it may not always be possible, try to avoid *it is* or *there is (are)* beginnings. Your sentences will be crisper and more concise:

orig There is little time remaining for the sales manager to reverse the financial trend.

rev Little time remains for the sales manager to reverse the financial trend.

orig It is certain that pollution will increase.

rev. Pollution will certainly increase.

BE FORCEFUL

Developing a forceful, vigorous style simply means learning some common tricks of the trade and practising them until they become habit.

Choose active over passive verbs

An active verb creates more energy than a passive one does:

> Active: She threw the ball.
>
> Passive: The ball was thrown by her.

Moreover, passive constructions tend to produce awkward, convoluted phrasing. Writers of bureaucratic documents are among the worst offenders:

> It <u>has been decided</u> that the utilization of small rivers in the province for purposes of generating hydro-electric power <u>should be studied</u> by our department and that a report to the Deputy <u>should be made</u> by our Director as soon as possible.

The passive verbs in this mouthful make it hard to tell who is doing what.

Passive verbs are appropriate in four instances:

1. When the subject is the passive recipient of some action:

> The cabinet minister <u>was heckled</u> by the angry crowd.

2. When you want to emphasize the object rather than the person acting:

> The anti-pollution devices in all three plants <u>will be improved</u>.

3. When you want to avoid an awkward shift of subject in a sentence or paragraph. Using the passive will sometimes help you maintain focus:

> The Jesuits began to convert the Hurons but <u>were attacked</u> by an Iroquois band before they had completed the mission.

4. When you want to avoid placing responsibility or blame:

> The plans <u>were delayed</u> when the proposer became ill.

When these exceptions don't apply, make an effort to use active verbs for a livelier style.

Use personal subjects

Most of us find it more interesting to learn about people than about things—hence the enduring appeal of the gossip columns. Wherever possible, therefore, make the subjects of your sentences personal. This trick goes hand-in-hand with use of active verbs. Almost any sentence becomes more lively with active verbs and a personal subject:

orig · The <u>outcome</u> of the union members' vote <u>was</u> the <u>decision</u> to resume work on Monday.

rev. The union <u>members voted</u> to return to work on Monday.

Here's another example:

orig It <u>can be assumed</u> that an <u>agreement was reached</u>, since <u>there were</u> smiles on both management and union sides when the <u>meeting was finished</u>.

rev <u>We can assume</u> that management and the union <u>reached</u> an agreement, since both <u>bargainers were smiling</u> when <u>they finished</u> the meeting.

(or)

rev Apparently <u>management and union reached</u> an agreement since, when <u>they finished</u> the meeting, both <u>bargainers were smiling</u>.

Use concrete details

Concrete details are easier to understand—and to remember—than abstract theories. Whenever you are discussing abstract concepts, therefore, always provide specific examples and illustrations; if you have a choice between a concrete word and an abstract one, choose the concrete. Consider this sentence:

> The French explored the northern territory and traded with the native people.

Now see how a few specific details can bring the facts to life:

> The French voyageurs paddled their way along the river systems of the north, trading their blankets and copper kettles for the Indians' furs.

Suggesting that you add concreteness doesn't mean getting rid of all abstractions. It's simply a plea to balance them with accurate details. Here is one instance in which added wording, if it is concrete and correct, can improve your writing.

Make important ideas stand out

Experienced writers know how to manipulate sentences in order to emphasize certain points. Here are some of their techniques:

Place key words in strategic positions

The positions of emphasis in a sentence are the beginning and, above all, the end. If you want to bring your point home with force, don't put the key words in the middle of the sentence. Save them for the last:

orig   People are less afraid of losing wealth than of losing face in this image-conscious society.

rev   In this image-conscious society, people are less afraid of losing wealth than of losing face.

Subordinate minor ideas

Small children connect incidents with a string of *and*s, as if everything were of equal importance:

> We went to the zoo and we saw a lion and John spilled his drink.

As they grow up, however, they learn to subordinate: that is, to make one part of a sentence less important in order to emphasize another point:

> Because the bus was delayed, we missed our class.

Major ideas stand out more and connections become clearer when minor ideas are subordinated:

orig   Night came and the ship slipped away from her captors.

rev   When night came, the ship slipped away from her captors.

Make your most important idea the subject of the main clause, and try to put it at the end, where it will be most emphatic:

orig   I was relieved when I saw my marks.

rev   When I saw my marks, I was relieved.

Vary sentence structure

As with anything else, variety adds spice to writing. One way of adding variety, which will also make an important idea stand out, is to use a periodic rather than a simple sentence structure.

Most sentences follow the simple pattern of subject—verb—object (plus modifiers):

> The <u>dog</u> <u>bit</u> the <u>man</u> on the ankle.
>   s   v   o

A *simple sentence* such as this gives the main idea at the beginning and therefore creates little tension. A *periodic sentence*, on the other hand, does not give the main clause until the end, following one or more subordinate clauses:

> Since he had failed to keep his promises or to inspire the voters, in the next election he <u>was defeated</u>.
>   s   v

The longer the periodic sentence is, the greater the suspense and the more emphatic the final part. Since this high-tension structure is more difficult to read than the simple sentence, your readers would be exhausted if you used it too often. Save it for those times when you want to create a special effect or play on emotions.

Vary sentence length

A short sentence can add punch to an important point, especially when it comes as a surprise. This technique can be particularly useful for conclusions. Don't overdo it, though. A string of long sentences may be monotonous, but a string of short ones has a staccato effect that can make your writing sound like a child's reader: "This is my dog. See him run."

Still, academic papers usually have too many long sentences rather than too many short ones. Since short sentences are easier to read, try breaking up clusters of long ones. Aim for variety.

Use contrast

Just as a jeweller will highlight a diamond by displaying it against dark velvet, so you can highlight an idea by placing it against a contrasting background:

orig. Most employees in industry do not have indexed pensions.

new. Unlike civil servants, most employees in industry do not have indexed pensions.

Using parallel phrasing will increase the effect of the contrast:

> Although he often spoke to business groups, he seldom spoke in Parliament.

Use a well-placed adverb or correlative construction

Adding an adverb or two can sometimes help you to dramatize a concept:

orig. Although I dislike the proposal, I must accept it as the practical answer.

rev. Athough emotionally I dislike the concept, intellectually I must accept it as the practical answer.

Correlatives such as *both . . . and* or *not only . . . but also* can be used to emphasize combinations as well:

orig. Smith was a good coach and a good friend.

rev. Smith was both a good coach and a good friend.

rev. Smith was not only a good coach but also a good friend.

Use repetition

Repetition is a highly effective emphatic device. It helps to stir the emotions:

> He fought injustice and corruption. He fought complacent politicians and inept policies. He fought hard, but he always fought fairly.

Of course, you would only use such a dramatic technique on rare occasions.

Use your ears

Your ears are probably your best critics: make good use of them. Before producing a final copy of any piece of writing, read it out loud, in a clear voice. The difference between cumbersome and fluent passages will be unmistakable.

Some final advice: write before you revise

No one would expect you to sit down and put all this advice into practice as soon as you start to write. You would feel so constrained that it would be hard to get anything down on paper at all. You will be better off if you begin practising these techniques during the editing process, when you are looking critically at what you have already written. Some experienced writers can combine the creative and critical functions, but most of us find it easier to write a rough draft first, before starting the detailed task of revising.

NOTE

[1]Discussion of focus and examples based on Robert Cluett and Lee Ahlborn, *Effective English Prose* (New York: L.W. Singer Co., 1965), 51.

9
COMMON ERRORS
in grammar and
usage

This chapter is not a comprehensive grammar lesson: it's simply a survey of those areas where students most often make mistakes. It will help you to keep a look-out for weaknesses as you are editing your work. Once you get into the habit of checking, it won't be long before you are correcting potential problems as you write.

The grammatical terms used here are the most simple and familiar ones; if you need to review some of them, see the Glossary. For a thorough treatment of grammar or usage, consult a complete text such as A.J. Thompson and A.V. Martinet's *A Practical English Grammar*, 3rd ed. (Oxford: Oxford University Press, 1980).

Troubles with sentence unity

Sentence fragments

To be complete, a sentence must have both a subject and a verb in an independent clause; if it doesn't, it's a fragment. Occasionally a sentence fragment is acceptable, as in

✓ Will the government try to abolish the Senate? <u>Not likely.</u>

Here the sentence fragment *not likely* is clearly intended to be understood as a short form of *It is not likely that it will try*. Unintentional sentence fragments, on the other hand, usually seem incomplete rather than shortened:

✗ I enjoy living in Vancouver. <u>Being a skier who likes the sea.</u>

The last ''sentence'' is incomplete: where is the subject or verb? (Remember that a participle such as *being* is not a verb; ''-ing'' words by themselves are only verbals or part-verbs.) The fragment can be made into a complete sentence by adding a subject and a verb:

✓ I <u>am</u> a skier who likes the sea.

Alternatively, you could join the fragment to the preceding sentence:

✓ Being a skier who likes the sea, I enjoy living in Vancouver.

✓ I enjoy living in Vancouver, since I am a skier who likes the sea.

Run-on sentences

A run-on sentence is one that continues beyond the point where it should have stopped:

✗ Mosquitoes and blackflies are annoying, but they don't stop tourists from coming to spend their holidays in Canada and such is the case in Ontario's northland.

The *and* should be dropped and a period or semicolon added after *Canada*.

Another kind of run-on sentence is one in which two independent clauses (phrases that could stand by themselves as sentences) are wrongly joined by a comma:

✗ Northrop Frye has won international acclaim as a critic, he is an English professor at the University of Toronto.

This error is known as a *comma splice*. There are three ways of correcting it:

• by putting a period after *critics* and starting a new sentence:

✓ . . . as a critic. He . . .

• by replacing the comma with a semicolon:

✓ . . . as a critic; he . . .

• by making one of the independent clauses subordinate to the other:

✓ Northrop Frye, who has won international acclaim as a critic, is an English professor at the University of Toronto.

The one exception to the rule that independent clauses cannot be joined by a comma arises when the clauses are very short and arranged in a tight sequence:

✓ I opened the door, I saw the skunk, I shut the door.

Such instances are obviously uncommon.

Contrary to what many people think, words such as *however*, *therefore*, and *thus* cannot be used to join independent clauses:

✗ Two of my friends started out in Commerce, however they quickly decided they didn't like accounting.

The mistake can be corrected by beginning a new sentence after *Commerce* or (preferably) by putting a semicolon in the same place:

✓ Two of my friends started out in Commerce; however, they quickly decided they didn't like accounting.

The only words that can be used to join independent clauses are the coordinating conjunctions—*and*, *or*, *nor*, *but*, *for*, *yet*, and *so*—and subordinating conjunctions such as *if*, *because*, *since*, *while*, *when*, *where*, *after*, *before*, and *until*.

Faulty predication

When the subject of a sentence is not grammatically connected to what follows (the predicate), the result is *faulty predication*:

✗ The <u>reason</u> for his downfall was <u>because</u> he couldn't handle people.

The problem is that *because* essentially means the same thing as *the reason for*. The subject needs a noun clause to complete it:

✓ The <u>reason</u> for his downfall was <u>that</u> he couldn't handle people.

Another solution would be to rephrase the sentence:

✓ He was defeated because he couldn't handle people.

Faulty predication also occurs with *is when* and *is where* constructions:

✗ The climax <u>is when</u> the servant discovers the body.

You an correct this error in one of two ways:
1. Follow the *is* with a noun phrase to complete the sentence:

(or)
✓ The climax is <u>the discovery of the body</u> by the servant.
✓ The climax is <u>the servant's discovery</u> of the body.

2. Change the verb:

√ The climax <u>occurs</u> when the servant discovers the body.

Troubles with subject-verb agreement

Identifying the subject

A verb should always agree in number with its subject. Sometimes, however, when the subject does not come at the beginning of the sentence, or when it is separated from the verb by other information, you may be tempted to use a verb form that does not agree:

X The <u>increase</u> in the rate for freight and passengers <u>were condemned</u> by the farmers.

The subject here is *increase*, not *freight and passengers*; therefore the verb should be the singular *was condemned*:

√ The <u>increase</u> in the rate for freight and passengers <u>was condemned</u> by the farmers.

Either, neither, each

The indefinite pronouns *either*, *neither*, and *each* always take singular verbs:

X <u>Neither</u> of the changing rooms <u>have</u> a sauna.

√ <u>Each</u> of them <u>has</u> a shower.

Compound subjects

When *or*, *either . . . or*, or *neither . . . nor* is used to create a compound subject, the verb should usually agree with the last item in the subject:

√ Neither my room-mate nor my <u>team-mates</u> <u>are going</u> home for the holiday.

If a singular item follows a plural item, however, a singular verb may sound awkward, and it's better to rephrase the sentence:

orig . Either my history <u>books</u> or my biology <u>text</u> <u>is going</u> to gather dust this weekend.

rev . This weekend, I'm going to leave behind either my history books or my biology text.

Unlike the word *and*, which creates a compound subject and therefore takes a plural verb, *as well as* or *in addition to* does not create a compound subject; therefore the verb remains singular:

✓ Tourtière <u>and</u> sugar-pie <u>are</u> traditional French-Canadian dishes.

✓ Tourtière <u>as well as</u> sugar-pie <u>is</u> a traditional French-Canadian dish.

Collective nouns

A collective noun is a singular noun, such as *family*, *army*, or *team*, that includes a number of members. If the noun refers to the members as a unit, it takes a singular verb:

✓ The <u>family goes</u> on holiday in June.

If the noun refers to the members as individuals, however, the verb becomes plural:

✓ The <u>team are receiving</u> their sweaters before the exhibition game.

✓ The <u>majority</u> of immigrants to Canada <u>settle</u> in cities.

Titles

A title is singular even if it contains plural words; therefore it takes a singular verb:

✓ <u>Tales of the South Pacific</u> was a best-seller.

✓ McCarthy and McCarthy is handling the court case.

Tense troubles

Native speakers of English usually know the correct sequence of verb tense by ear, but a few tenses can still be confusing.

The past perfect

If the main verb is in the past tense and you want to refer to something before that time, use the past perfect (*had* plus the past participle). The time sequence will not be clear if you use the simple past in both clauses:

✗ He hoped that she <u>bought</u> the typewriter.

✓ He hoped that she <u>had bought</u> the typewriter.

Similarly, when you are reporting what someone said in the past—
that is, when you are using past indirect discourse—you should use
the past perfect tense in the clause describing what was said:

X He said that the party <u>caused</u> the neighbours to complain.

✓ He said that the party <u>had caused</u> the neighbours to
complain.

Using "if"

When you are describing a possibility in the future, use the present
tense in the condition (*if*) clause and the future tense in the consequence clause:

✓ If he <u>tests</u> us on French verbs, I <u>will fail</u>.

When the possibility is unlikely, it is conventional—especially in
formal writing—to use the subjunctive in the *if* clause, and *would* plus
the base verb in the consequence clause:

✓ If he <u>were to cancel</u> the test, I <u>would cheer</u>.

When you are describing a hypothetical instance in the past, use
the past subjunctive (it has the same form as the past perfect) in the *if*
clause and *would have* plus the past participle for the consequence.
A common error is to use *would have* in both clauses:

X If she <u>would have been</u> more friendly, I <u>would have asked</u>
her to dance.

✓ If she <u>had been</u> more friendly, I <u>would have asked</u> her to
dance.

Writing about literature

When you are describing a literary work in its historical context, use
the past tense:

✓ Margaret Atwood <u>wrote</u> <u>Surfacing</u> at a time when George
Grant's <u>Technology and Empire</u> <u>was persuading</u> people to
reassess technocratic values.

To discuss what goes on *within* a work of literature, however, you
should use the present tense:

✓ The narrator <u>retreats</u> to the woods and <u>tries</u> to escape the
rationalism of her father's world.

When you are discussing an episode or incident in a literary work and want to refer to a prior incident or a future one, use past or future tenses accordingly:

✓ The narrator returns to northern Quebec, where she <u>spent</u> her summers as a child; by the time she leaves, she <u>will have rediscovered</u> herself.

Be sure to return to the present tense when you have finished referring to events in the past or future.

Pronoun troubles

Pronoun reference

The link between a pronoun and the noun it refers to must be clear. If the noun doesn't appear in the same sentence as the pronoun, it should appear in the preceding sentence:

✗ The textbook supply in the bookstore had run out, and so we borrowed <u>them</u> from the library.

Since *textbook* is used as an adjective rather than a noun, it cannot serve as referent or antecedent for the pronoun *them*. You must either replace *them* or change the phrase *textbook supply*.

✓ The <u>textbook supply</u> in the bookstore had run out, and so we borrowed the <u>texts</u> from the library.

✓ The <u>textbooks</u> in the bookstore had run out, and so we borrowed <u>them</u> from the library.

When a sentence contains more than one noun, make sure there is no ambiguity about which noun the pronoun refers to:

✗ The public wants increased social <u>services</u> as well as lower <u>taxes,</u> but the government does not advocate <u>them</u>.

What does the pronoun *them* refer to? The taxes, the social services, or both?

✓ The public wants <u>increased</u> social <u>services</u> as well as lower taxes, but the government does not advocate such <u>increases</u>.

Using "it" and "this"

Using *it* and *this* without a clear referent can lead to confusion:

✗ Although the directors wanted to meet in January, <u>it</u> (<u>this</u>) didn't take place until May.

✓ Although the directors wanted to meet in January, <u>the conference</u> didn't take place until May.

Make sure that *it* or *this* clearly refers to a specific noun or pronoun.

Pronoun agreement—and sex

A pronoun should agree in number and person with the noun that it refers to:

X When a Canadian civil <u>servant</u> retires, <u>their</u> pension is indexed.

✓ When a Canadian civil <u>servant</u> retires, <u>his</u> pension is indexed.

This mistake increasingly occurs because writers are reluctant to use the traditional "he" to refer to both sexes. Many language experts still maintain that this pronoun has a dual meaning, one for an individual male and one for any human. Others claim that the traditional usage is sexist.

There's no easy answer that will satisfy both sides in this dispute. On the one hand, it's best to avoid using language that may offend some as sexist. On the other hand, "his/her" is intrusive and awkward. Probably the most acceptable solution for now is to try to change the singular noun to the plural:

✓ When Canadian civil <u>servants</u> retire, <u>their pensions</u> are indexed.

You can also use the occasional "he or she," as this book does. Whatever form you choose, check for agreement. And at least try to make clear in your examples and illustrations that you are referring to females as well as males. In addition, use neutral nouns whenever possible—for example, *sales agent* rather than *salesman*, or *flight attendant* rather than *stewardess*.

Using "one"

People often use the word *one* to avoid over-using *I* in their writing. Although in Britain this is common, in Canada and the United States frequent use of *one* may seem too formal and even a bit pompous:

If <u>one</u> were to apply for the grant, <u>one</u> would find oneself engulfed in so many bureaucratic forms that <u>one's</u> patience would be stretched thin.

As a way out, it's becoming increasingly common in North America to use the third person *his* or *her* as the adjectival form of *one*:

<u>One</u> would find <u>his</u> patience stretched thin.

In any case, try to use *one* sparingly, and don't be afraid of the occasional *I*. The one serious error to avoid is mixing the third person *one* with the second person *you*:

X When <u>one</u> visits the Rockies, <u>you</u> are impressed by the grandeur of the scenery.

In formal academic writing generally, *you* is not an appropriate substitute for *one*.

Using "me" and other objective pronouns

Remembering that it's wrong to say "Jane and me were invited to the party," rather than "Jane and I were invited," many people use the subjective form of the pronoun even when it should be objective:

X He invited Jane and <u>I</u> to the party.

✓ He invited Jane and <u>me</u> to the party.

The verb *invited* requires an object, and *me* is the objective case. Here's a simple hint: read the sentence with only the problem pronoun. You will know by ear which form is correct:

He invited <u>me</u> to the party.

Prepositions should also be followed by the objective case:

X <u>Between</u> you and <u>I</u>, Brown is a bore.

✓ <u>Between</u> you and <u>me</u>, Brown is a bore.

X Eating well is a problem <u>for we</u> students.

✓ Eating well is a problem <u>for us</u> students.

There are times, however, when the correct case can sound stiff or awkward:

orig. To whom was the award given?

Rather than keeping to a correct but awkward form, try to reword the sentence:

rev. Who received the award?

Exceptions for pronouns following prepositions

The rule that a pronoun following a preposition takes the objective case has exceptions. When the preposition is followed by a clause, the pronoun should take the case required by its position in the clause:

X   The Chairman showed some concern over <u>whom would be
      selected</u> as Dean.

Although the pronoun follows the preposition *over*, it is also the subject
of the verb *would be selected* and therefore requires the subjective case:

✓   The Chairman showed some concern over <u>who would be
      selected</u> as Dean.

Similarly, when a gerund (a word that acts partly as a noun and
partly as a verb) is the subject of a clause, the pronoun that modifies it
takes the possessive case:

X   Mother was elated by <u>him marrying</u> the Mayor's daughter.

✓   Mother was elated by <u>his marrying</u> the Mayor's daughter.

Troubles with modifying

Adjectives modify nouns; adverbs modify verbs, adjectives, and other
adverbs. Do not use an adjective to modify a verb:

X   He played <u>good</u>. (Adjective with verb)
✓   He played <u>well</u>. (Adverb modifying verb)
✓   He played <u>really well</u>. (Adverb modifying adverb)
✓   He had a <u>good style</u>. (Adjective modifying noun)
✓   He had a <u>really good</u> style. (Adverb modifying adjective)

Squinting modifiers

Remember that clarity largely depends on word order: to avoid
confusion, the relations between the different parts of a sentence must
be clear. Modifiers should therefore be as close as possible to the words
they modify. A *squinting modifier* is one that, because of its position,
seems to look in two directions at once:

X   She expected <u>in the spring</u> a decline in the stock market.

Was *spring* the time of expectation or the time of the market decline?
The logical relation is usually clearest when you place the modifier
immediately in front of the element it modifies:

✓   <u>In the spring</u> she <u>expected</u> a decline in the stock market.

✓   She expected a <u>spring decline</u> in the stock market.

Other squinting modifiers can be corrected in the same way:

X   Our English professor gave a lecture on <u>Beowulf</u>, <u>which
      was well illustrated</u>.

✓ Our English professor gave a <u>well-illustrated lecture</u> on Beowulf.

Dangling modifiers

Modifiers that have no grammatical connection with anything else in the sentence are said to be *dangling*:

✗ <u>Walking</u> around the campus in June, the river and trees made a picturesque scene.

Who is doing the walking? Here's another example:

✗ <u>Reflecting</u> on the results of the referendum, it was decided not to press for independence for a while.

Who is doing the reflecting? Clarify the meaning by connecting the dangling modifier to a new subject:

✓ <u>Walking</u> around the campus in June, <u>she</u> thought the river and trees made a picturesque scene.

✓ <u>Reflecting</u> on the results of the referendum, <u>they</u> decided not to press for independence for a while.

Troubles with pairs (and more)

Comparisons

Make sure that your comparisons are complete. The second element in a comparison should be equivalent to the first, whether the equivalence is stated or merely implied:

✗ Today's students have a greater understanding of calculus than their parents.

This sentence suggests that the two things being compared are *calculus* and *parents*. Adding a second verb (*have*) equivalent to the first one shows that the two things being compared are *parents' understanding* and *students' understanding*:

✓ Today's students <u>have</u> a greater understanding of calculus than their parents <u>have</u>.

A similar problem arises in the following comparison:

✗ That cabinet minister is <u>a tiresome man</u> and so are his press conferences.

Press conferences may be tiresome, but they are not *a tiresome man*; to make sense, the two parts of the comparison must be parallel:

✓ That cabinet minister is <u>tiresome</u>, and so are his press conferences.

Correlatives (coordinate constructions)

Constructions such as *both . . . and*, *not only . . . but*, and *neither . . . nor* are especially tricky. The coordinating term must not come too early, or else one of the parts that come after will not connect with the common element. For the implied comparison to work, the two parts that come after the coordinating term must be grammatically equivalent:

✗ He <u>not only</u> bakes cakes <u>but</u> bread.

✓ He bakes <u>not only</u> cakes <u>but</u> bread.

Parallel phrasing

A series of items in a sentence should be phrased in parallel wording. Make sure that all the parts of a parallel construction are in fact equal:

✗ Mackenzie King loved <u>his</u> job, <u>his</u> dogs, and mother.

✓ Mackenzie King loved <u>his</u> job, <u>his</u> dogs, and <u>his</u> mother.

Once you have decided to include the pronoun *his* in the first two elements, the third must have it too.

For clarity as well as stylistic grace, keep similar ideas in similar form:

✗ He <u>failed</u> Economics and <u>barely passed</u> Statistics, but Political Science <u>was</u> a subject he did well in.

✓ He <u>failed</u> Economics and <u>barely passed</u> Statistics, but <u>did well</u> in Political Science.

10
PUNCTUATION

Punctuation causes students so many problems that it deserves a chapter of its own. If your punctuation is faulty, your readers will be confused and may have to backtrack; worse still, they may be tempted to skip over the rough spots. Punctuation marks are the traffic signals of writing; use them with precision to keep readers moving smoothly through your work.

PERIOD [.]

1. Use a period at the end of a sentence. A period indicates a full stop, not just a pause.

2. Use a period with abbreviations. British style omits the period in certain cases, but North American style usually requires it for abbreviated titles (Mrs., Dr., etc.) as well as place-names (B.C., N.W.T., etc.). Although the abbreviations and acronyms for some organizations include periods, the most common ones generally do not (CARE, CIDA, etc.).

3. Use a period at the end of an indirect question. Do *not* use a question mark:

    X He asked if I wanted a substitute?

    ✓ He asked if I wanted a substitute.

4. Use a period for questions that are really polite orders:

    Will you please send him the report by Friday.

COMMA [,]

Commas are the trickiest of all punctuation marks: even the experts differ on when to use them. Most agree, however, that too many commas are as bad as too few, since they make writing choppy and awkward to read. Certainly recent writers use fewer commas than earlier stylists did. Whenever you are in doubt, let clarity be your guide. The most widely accepted conventions are these:

1. Use a comma to separate two independent clauses joined by a coordinating conjunction (and, but, for, or, nor, yet, so). By signalling that there are two clauses, the comma will prevent the reader from confusing the beginning of the second clause with the end of the first:

  ✗ He went out for dinner with his sister and his room-mate joined them later.

  ✓ He went out for dinner with his sister, and his room-mate joined them later.

When the second clause has the same subject as the first, you have the option of omitting both the second subject and the comma:

  ✓ He can stick-handle well, but he can't shoot.

  ✓ He can stick-handle well but can't shoot.

If you mistakenly punctuate two sentences as if they were one, the result will be a *run-on sentence*; if you use a comma but forget the coordinating conjunction, the result will be a *comma splice*:

  ✗ He took his family to the zoo, it was closed for repairs.

  ✓ He took his family to the zoo, but it was closed for repairs.

Remember that words such as *however*, *therefore*, and *thus* are *conjunctive adverbs*, not conjunctions: if you use one of them the way you would use a conjunction, the result will again be a *comma splice*:

  ✗ She was accepted into medical school, however, she took a year off to earn her tuition.

  ✓ She was accepted into medical school; however, she took a year off to earn her tuition.

Conjunctive adverbs are often confused with conjunctions. You can distinguish between the two if you remember that a conjunctive adverb's position in a sentence can be changed:

    She was accepted into medical school; she took a year off, <u>however</u>, to earn her tuition.

The position of a conjunction, on the other hand, is invariable; it must be placed between the two clauses:

    She was accepted into medical school, <u>but</u> she took a year off to earn her tuition.

When, in rare cases, the independent clauses are short and closely related, they may be joined by a comma alone:

✓ I came, I saw, I conquered.

A *fused sentence* is a run-on sentence in which independent clauses are slapped together with no punctuation at all:

✗ He watched the hockey game all afternoon the only exercise he got was going to the kitchen between periods.

A fused sentence sounds like breathless babbling—and it's a serious error.

2. Use a comma between items in a series. (Place a coordinating conjunction before the last item):

> She finally found an apartment that was large, bright, and clean.

> Then she had to scrounge around for dishes, pots, cutlery, and a kettle.

The comma before the conjunction is optional:

> She kept a cat, a dog and a budgie.

Sometimes, however, the final comma can help to prevent confusion:

> When we set off on our trip, we were warned about passport thieves, attacks on single women, and baggage loss.

In this case, the comma prevents the reader from thinking that *attacks* are made on *baggage* as well as *single women*.

3. Use a comma to separate adjectives preceding a noun when they modify the same element:

> It was a rainy, windy night.

When the adjectives *do not* modify the same element, however, you should not use a comma:

> It was a pleasant winter outing.

Here *winter* modifies *outing*, but *pleasant* modifies the total phrase *winter outing*. A good way of checking whether or not you need a comma is to see if you can reverse the order of the adjectives. If you can reverse it (*rainy, windy night* or *windy, rainy night*), use a comma; if you can't (*winter pleasant outing*), omit the comma.

4. Use commas to set off an interruption (an interrupting word or phrase is technically called a parenthetical element):

✓ The film, I hear, isn't nearly as good as the book.

✓ My tutor, however, couldn't answer the question.

Remember to put commas on *both sides* of the interruption:

✗ The music, they say was adapted from a piece by Mozart.

✓ The music, they say, was adapted from a piece by Mozart.

5. Use commas to set off words or phrases that provide additional but non-essential information:

Our president, Sue Stephens, does her job well.

The black retriever, his closest companion, went with him everywhere.

Sue Stephens and *his closest companion* are *appositives*: they give additional information about the nouns they refer to (*president* and *retriever*), but the sentences would be understandable without them. Here's another example:

My oldest friend, who lives in Halifax, was married last week.

The phrase *who lives in Halifax* is called a *non-restrictive* modifier, because it does not limit the meaning of the word it modifies (*friend*). Without that modifying clause the sentence would still specify who was married. Since the information the clause provides is not necessary to the meaning of the sentence, you must use commas on both sides to set it off.

In contrast, a *restrictive* modifier is one that provides essential information; therefore it must not be set apart from the element it modifies, and commas should not be used:

The man who came to dinner was my uncle.

Without the clause *who came to dinner*, the reader would not know which man was the uncle.

To avoid confusion, be sure to distinguish carefully between essential and additional information. The difference can be important:

Students, who are not willing to work, should not receive grants.

Students who are not willing to work should not receive grants.

6. Use a comma after an introductory phrase when omitting it would cause confusion:

X   On the balcony above the singers entertained the diners.

✓   On the balcony above, the singers entertained the diners.

X   When he turned away the prisoner disappeared.

✓   When he turned away, the prisoner disappeared.

7. Use a comma to separate elements in dates and addresses:

> February 2, 1983. (Commas are often omitted if the day comes first: 2 February 1983)
>
> 117 Hudson Drive, Edmonton, Alberta.
>
> They lived in Dartmouth, Nova Scotia.

8. Use a comma before a quotation in a sentence:

> He said, "Life is too short to worry."
>
> "The children's safety," he warned, "is in your hands."

For more formality, you may use a colon (see p. 108).

9. Use a comma with a name followed by a title:

> D. Gunn, Ph.D.
>
> Alice Smith, M.D.

SEMICOLON [;]

1. Use a semicolon to join independent clauses (complete sentences) that are closely related:

> For five days he worked non-stop; by Saturday he was exhausted.
>
> His lecture was confusing; no one could understand the terminology.

A semicolon is especially useful when the second independent clause begins with a conjunctive adverb such as *however, moreover, consequently, nevertheless, in addition,* or *therefore* (usually followed by a comma):

> He bought a bag of doughnuts; however, none of the group was hungry.

Some grammarians may disagree, but it's usually acceptable to follow a semicolon with a coordinating conjunction if the second clause is complicated by other commas:

> John, my cousin, is a keen jogger in all weather; but sometimes, especially in winter, I think it does him more harm than good.

2. Use a semicolon to mark the divisions in a complicated series when individual items themselves need commas. Using a comma to mark the subdivisions and a semicolon to mark the main divisions will help to prevent mix-ups:

> X   He invited Prof. Brooks, the vice-principal, Jane Hunter, and John Taylor.

Is the vice-principal a separate person?

> ✓   He invited Prof. Brooks, the vice-principal; Jane Hunter; and John Taylor.

In a case such as this, the elements separated by the semicolon need not be independent clauses.

COLON [:]

A colon indicates that something is to follow.

1. Use a colon before a formal statement or series:

> The winners are the following: Jane, George, and Hugh.

Do not use a colon if the words preceding it do not form a complete sentence:

> X   The winners are: Jane, George and Hugh.
> ✓   The winners are Jane, George, and Hugh.

Occasionally, however, a colon is used if the list is arranged vertically:

> The winners are: Jane
>   George
>   Hugh

2. Use a colon for formality before a direct quotation:

> The leaders of the anti-nuclear group repeated their message: "The world needs bread before bombs."

DASH [--]

A dash creates an abrupt pause, emphasizing the words that follow. (Never use dashes as casual substitutes for other punctuation: overuse can detract from the calm, well-reasoned effect you want.)

1. Use a dash to stress a word or phrase:

The British--as a matter of honour--vowed to retake the islands.

Foster was well received in the legislature--at first.

2. Use a dash in interrupted or unfinished dialogue:

"It's a matter--to put it delicately--of personal hygiene."

In typing, use two hyphens together, with no spaces on either side, to show a dash.

EXCLAMATION MARK [!]

An exclamation mark helps to show emotion or feeling. It is usually found in dialogue:

"Woe is me!" she mourned.

In academic writing, you should use it only in those rare cases when you want to give a point an emotional emphasis:

He concluded that inflation would decrease in 1981. Some forecast!

QUOTATION MARKS [" " or ' ']

Quotation marks are usually double in American style and single in British. In Canada either is accepted—just be consistent.

1. Use quotation marks to signify direct discourse (the actual words of a speaker):

I asked, "What is the matter?"

He said, "I have a pain in my big toe."

2. Use quotation marks to show that words themselves are the issue:

The term "love" in tennis comes from the French word for "egg."

Alternatively, you may italicize or underline the terms in question.

Sometimes quotation marks are used to mark a slang word or an inappropriate usage, to show that the writer is aware of the difficulty:

Hitler's "final solution" was the most barbaric act of this century.

Use this device only when necessary; usually it's better to let the context show your attitude, or to choose another term.

3. Use quotation marks to enclose the titles of poems, short stories, paintings, songs, films, and articles in books or journals. In contrast, titles of books, paintings, or music are italicized or underlined:

> The story I like best in Robert Weaver's <u>Canadian Short Stories</u> is "Bernadette" by Mavis Gallant.

4. Use quotation marks to enclose quotations within quotations (single or double depending on your primary style):

> He said, "Hitler's 'final solution' was the most barbaric act of this century."

PLACEMENT OF PUNCTUATION WITH QUOTATION MARKS

Both the British and the American practices are accepted in Canada. British style usually places the punctuation outside the quotation marks, unless it is actually part of the quotation. The American practice, followed in this book, is increasingly common in Canada:

- A comma or period always goes inside the quotation marks:

> He said, "Give me another chance," but I replied, "You've had enough chances."

- A semicolon or colon always goes outside the quotation marks:

> George wants to watch "Second City"; I'd rather watch the hockey game.

- A question mark, dash, or exclamation mark goes inside quotation marks if it is part of the quotation, but outside if it is not:

> He asked, "What is for dinner?"
>
> Did he really call the boss a "lily-livered hypocrite"?
>
> His speech was hardly an appeal for "blood, sweat and tears"!
>
> I was just whispering to Mary, "That instructor is a--" when suddenly he glanced at me.

- When a reference is given parenthetically (in round brackets) at the end of a quotation, the quotation marks precede the parentheses and the sentence punctuation follows them:

> Lipsey suggests that we should "abandon the Foreign Investment Review Agency" (<u>Globe and Mail</u>, 12 April 1983).

APOSTROPHE [']

The apostrophe forms the possessive case for nouns and some pronouns. (Remember that possession may also be shown without an apostrophe if the possessor is preceded by *of*: *the thesis of McLuhan, the end of the day*.)

1. **Add an apostrophe followed by "s" to**
   - all singular and plural nouns *not* ending in *s*: *cat's, women's*.
   - singular *proper* nouns ending in *s*: *Keats's, Sis's* (but note that the final *s* can be omitted if the word has a number of them already and would sound awkward, as in *Jesus'* or certain classical names).
   - indefinite pronouns: *someone's, anybody's*, etc.;

2. **Add an apostrophe to plural nouns ending in "s"**: *families', houses', cars'*.

3. **Use an apostrophe to show contractions of words**: *isn't, can't, winter of '87*. Caution: don't confuse *it's* (the contraction of *it is*) with the possessive of *it — its —* which has no apostrophe.

PARENTHESES [( )]

1. **Use parentheses to enclose an explanation, example, or qualification.** Parentheses show that the enclosed material is of incidental importance to the main idea. They make a less pronounced interruption than a dash, but a more pronounced one than a comma:

> My wife (the eldest of five children) is a superb cook and carpenter.

> His latest plan (according to neighbours) is to dam the creek.

Remember that although punctuation should not precede parentheses, it may follow them if required by the sense of the sentence:

> I like coffee in the morning (if it's not instant), but she prefers tea.

If the parenthetical statement comes between two complete sentences, it should be punctuated as a sentence, with the period inside the parentheses:

> I finished my last essay on April 30. (It was on Aristotle's ethics.) Fortunately, I had three weeks free to study for the exam.

2. **Use parentheses to enclose references.** See Chapter 11 for details.

BRACKETS [ ]

Brackets are square enclosures, not to be confused with parentheses (which are round).

1. Use brackets to set off a remark of your own within a quotation.
They show that the words enclosed are not those of the person quoted:

> Fox maintains, "Obstacles to western unification [in the eighties] are as many as they are serious."

Brackets are sometimes used to enclose *sic* (Latin for *thus*), which is used after an error, such as a misspelling, to show that the mistake was in the original. *Sic* should be underlined:

> The politician, in his letter to constitutents, wrote about "these parlouse [sic] times of economic difficulty."

HYPHEN [-]

1. Use a hyphen if you must divide a word at the end of a line.
When a word is too long to fit at the end of a line, it's best to keep it in one piece by starting a new line. If you must divide, however, remember these rules:
- Divide between syllables.
- Never divide a one-syllable word.
- Never leave one letter by itself.
- Divide double consonants except when they come before a suffix, in which case divide before the suffix:

> ar-rangement
> embar-rassment
> fall-ing
> pass-able

When the second consonant has been added to form the suffix, keep it with the suffix:

> refer-ral
> begin-ning

2. Use a hyphen to separate the parts of certain compound words:

> sister-in-law, vice-consul (compound nouns)

> test-drive, proof-read (compound verbs)

> well-considered plan, twentieth-century attitudes
> (compound adjectives used as modifiers preceding nouns)

When you are *not* using such expressions adjectivally, do *not* hyphenate them:

> The plan was well considered.
> These are attitudes of the twentieth century.

After long-time use, some compound nouns drop the hyphen. When in doubt, check a dictionary.

3. Use a hyphen with certain prefixes (*all-*, *self-*, *ex-*, and those prefixes preceding a proper name):

> all-party, self-imposed, ex-jockey, anti-nuclear, pro-Canadian.

4. Use a hyphen to emphasize contrasting prefixes:

> The coach agreed to give both pre- and post-game interviews.

5. Use a hyphen to separate written-out compound numbers from one to a hundred and compound fractions used as modifiers:

> eighty-one years ago
> seven-tenths full

6. Use a hyphen to separate parts of inclusive numbers or dates:

> the years 1890-1914
> pages 3-40

ELLIPSIS [. . .]

1. Use an ellipsis to show an omission from a quotation:

> He reported that "the drought in the thirties, to many farming families in the west . . . resembled a biblical plague, even to the locusts."

If the omission comes at the end of a sentence, the ellipsis is followed by a fourth period.

2. Use an ellipsis to show that a series of numbers continues indefinitely:

> 1, 3, 5, 7, 9 ...

ITALICS [*italics*] OR UNDERLINING

Italics are slanted (cursive) letters. Since many typewriters and word-processors don't have the mechanism for italics, underlining is an acceptable substitute.

1. Use italics for the titles of books, long poems that are complete books, plays, films, and lengthy musical pieces:

Davies's Fifth Business is one of my favourite novels.

Note: for articles, essays, and short poems or musical pieces, use quotation marks. If the title contains another title, be sure to set it off in the correct style:

- When both titles are books (or book-length), use quotation marks for the internal one:

  Her latest book is A Modern Reading of ''Hamlet.''

- When the internal title is a book but the main title is not, use italics (underlining):

  For more detail, see his article, ''The Perception of Advertising in McLuhan's Understanding Media.''

- When neither title is a book, use the alternate form of quotation marks:

  Her essay is entitled ''Imagery in Keats's 'To Autumn.' ''

2. Use italics to emphasize an idea:

It is important that all equipment be washed immediately.

Be sparing with this use, interspersing it with other, less intrusive methods of creating emphasis.

3. Use italics (or quotation marks) to emphasize a word as a word:

The term peer group is an example of sociological jargon.

4. Use italics for foreign words or expressions:

The final sentence of her argument is a non sequitur.

11
DOCUMENTATION
in the humanities

This chapter is specifically intended as a guide for handling quotations, footnotes, and bibliographies in humanities subjects; however, it may also be useful for some subjects in the social sciences.

QUOTATIONS

Quotations can add authority to your writing as well as help you avoid charges of plagiarism. But you should use them with care: never quote a passage just because it sounds impressive. Be sure that it really adds to your discussion, either by expressing an idea with special force or cogency, or by giving substance to a debatable point.

Guidelines for incorporating quotations

1. Integrate the quotation so that it makes sense in the context of your discussion and fits grammatically into a sentence:

   ✗ Henry Ford had little knowledge of history. "History is bunk," but his opinion is not one that many educated people would accept.

   ✓ Henry Ford had little knowledge of history. His opinion that "history is bunk" is not one that many educated people would accept.

2. Be accurate. Reproduce the exact wording, punctuation, and spelling of the original, including any errors. You can acknowledge a mistake by inserting the Latin word *sic* in brackets after it (see p. 112). If you want to underline part of the quotation for emphasis, add *my emphasis* in brackets at the end.

3. Include as part of your text, enclosed in quotation marks,
   - not more than four lines of prose;
   - not more than three lines of verse. Use a slash(/) to indicate the end of a line:

   > When Keats says, "That I may drink, and leave the world
   > unseen/And with thee fade away into the forest dim," he
   > is referring to the temptations of death.

4. Set off from your text by indenting (five to ten spaces) and omitting quotation marks
   - five or more lines of prose;
   - four or more lines of verse.

   A long quotation is usually single-spaced and introduced by a colon. If the first line of your quotation is the first sentence of a new paragraph, indent the first line an extra three spaces:

   > Machiavelli recognized the ability of a republic to change
   > with the times:
   >> Therefore, the truth is that a republic is of longer
   >> duration and has a much better fortune than a princi-
   >> pality, for a republic, by virtue of its diverse citizenry,
   >> can better accommodate itself to the changeability
   >> of conditions than can a prince.

5. For a quotation within a quotation, use single quotation marks:

   > A news report described the scene this way: "When the
   > crowd heard de Gaulle shout, 'Vive le Québec libre!', they
   > roared with approval."

6. If you want to omit something from the original, use ellipsis marks (three single-spaced periods):

   > "The uprising was the result of indifference on the part of
   > national leaders . . . and mismanagement on the part of
   > civil servants."

If the omission is at the end of a sentence, add a fourth period.
To omit a full line of a poem, use a full line of single-spaced periods:

> Cedar and jagged fir
> . . . .
> against the gray
> and cloud-piled sky

7. If you want to insert an explanatory comment of your own into a quotation, enclose it in square brackets:

> "At private meetings, three western premiers [Bennett, Lougheed, and Devine] strenuously objected to the federal proposal."

Note that brackets are square, not round; if your typewriter doesn't have a key for brackets, mark them by hand.

TRADITIONAL HUMANITIES DOCUMENTATION

This traditional approach uses both footnotes (or endnotes) and a bibliography.

Footnotes

Footnotes allow the reader to check sources and verify information. If you are quoting or summarizing other people's ideas, you also need them to avoid charges of plagiarism. But having too many notes can interrupt the reader's progress. To avoid clutter, remember that you don't need references to common knowledge or undisputed facts. As well, try to include in the text as much as you can of the footnote information, keeping the note itself as short as possible.

Use footnotes in four specific instances:

- to identify or document quotations;
- to acknowledge and give exact references to the words and ideas of others—even if you paraphrase or summarize them in your own words, rather than quote directly;
- to provide additional relevant information or comments that are difficult to fit into the text;
- to refer to other parts of a long discussion.

Format

1. For the reader's convenience, you may place your footnote at the bottom of the page on which the citation appears. Be sure to leave enough space; don't cram it into the margin at the bottom of the page. You should also leave a quadruple space between the text and the footnote, to make the division clear.
2. If you choose to place all your footnotes at the end of your writing you may call them *endnotes*. Using a separate page, underline your title—*Footnotes* or *Endnotes*—and centre the notes under it. Leave a triple space between the title and the first entry.

3. Whichever format you choose, remember to number your notes consecutively, using arabic numerals, and to put the corresponding number at the end of the sentence in which you make each reference, using superscript (a number slightly raised above the line of words). The numbers should follow all end punctuation.

4. Bottom-of-the-page footnotes should be indented the same number of spaces that you use for a new paragraph. In student writing, they should be single-spaced, in contrast to the double-spaced text. Leave a double space between entries.

The following examples of documentation are restricted to the most common kinds of footnote and bibliographic references. For a more comprehensive survey, consult one of the following:

- *MLA Handbook for Writers of Research Papers, Theses, and Dissertations* (New York: Modern Language Association, 1984).
- Kate Turabian, *A Manual for Writers of Term Papers, Theses, and Dissertations,* 3rd ed., rev. (Chicago: Univ. of Chicago Press, 1967).
- Roy Wiles, *Scholarly Reporting in the Humanities*, 4th ed., rev. (Toronto: Univ. of Toronto Press, 1972).

Footnotes for first references

Book by one author:

[1]Desmond Morton, <u>Ministers and Generals: Politics and the Canadian Militia</u> (Toronto: Univ. of Toronto Press, 1970), 20.

Capitalize the first letter in the title and subtitle, as well as the first letters of all words except for articles, prepositions, and conjunctions. If you give full bibliographic references later, you may omit subtitles in notes. Familiar terms such as *University* or *editor* may be abbreviated.

Book by two authors:

[2]Clara Thomas and John Lennox, <u>William Arthur Deacon: A Canadian Literary Life</u> (Toronto: Univ. of Toronto Press, 1982), 32.

Although the title page may list more than one place of publication (say, Toronto and Buffalo), you need only name the first place in your reference.

Book by three or more authors:

[3]Richard G. Lipsey et al., <u>Economics</u>, 4th ed. (New York: Harper and Row, 1982), 67.

Edition other than the first:

> ⁴Paul W. Fox, ed., Politics: Canada, 4th ed. (Toronto: McGraw-Hill Ryerson, 1977), 3.

Book with one editor:

> ⁵Germaine Warkentin, ed., Stories from Ontario: A Selection (Toronto: Macmillan, 1974).

When the publisher's full title is lengthy, you may use its familiar short form; thus *Macmillan of Canada Ltd.* becomes simply *Macmillan*.

Book with two editors:

> ⁶Ralph Kruyeger and R. Charles Bryfogle, eds., Urban Problems (Toronto: Holt, 1971).

Books by one author edited by another:

> ⁷Hugh MacLennan, The Other Side of Hugh MacLennan, Elspeth Cameron, ed. (Toronto: Macmillan, 1978).

Books by one author translated by another:

> ⁸Plato's Republic, G.M.A. Grube, trans. (Indianapolis: Huckett, 1974).

You need not list the author's name when it is part of the title.

Book in more than one volume:

> ⁹Donald Creighton, John A. Macdonald (Toronto: Macmillan, 1955-56), 2 vols.

Article by one author in a work edited by another:

> ¹⁰Michael Hornyansky, "Is Your English Destroying Your Image?" in In the Name of Language, Joseph Gold, ed. (Toronto: Macmillan, 1975).

Article in a journal with separate issues:

> ¹¹Jeffrey M. Heath, "The Private Language of Evelyn Waugh," English Studies in Canada 2, no. 3 (Fall 1976), 329-39.

The abbreviations *p.* or *pp.* may be used to indicate page numbers, but increasingly they are omitted from references. Most page numbers may be contracted to avoid unnecessary repetition (for example, *33-7, 465-82, 1277-9*); however, numbers between *10* and *20* should always be written in full (*10-11, 12-15, 214-18, 1342-1480*). If the issue of the journal in which the article appears is one of several bound together to form a single volume with continuous page numbers, you may leave out the week or month of publication. Just give the volume number, year (in parentheses), and page numbers:

[1]George Woodcock, "Anarchist Phases and Personalities," Queen's Quarterly 87 (1980), 82-97.

Unsigned article in an encyclopedia:

[12]Encyclopaedia Britannica: Micropaedia, 1974 ed., s.v. "Riel, Louis".

When citing entries in dictionaries and other unsigned, alphabetically arranged reference books, it's best to use *s.v.* (*sub verbo*, "under the word") rather than the volume and page numbers.

When an entry is signed, list the author's name first.

Government document:

[13]Canada Dept. of Labour, Women's Bureau, Changing Patterns in Women's Employment (Ottawa: Queen's Printer, 1966), 70.

Proceedings:

[14]Canadian Institute of International Affairs, Proceedings of Lester B. Pearson Conference on Canada-United States Relationship (Niagara-on-the-Lake, Ont.: n.p., 1976), 32.

The abbreviation *n.p.* indicates that there is no publisher.

Book review:

[15]Grant Reuber, rev. of On Economics and Society by Harry G. Johnson, Queen's Quarterly 83, no. 1 (Spring 1976), 129-30.

Signed newspaper article:

[16]Robert Gibbens, "Quebec Government Reviews Equipment Purchasing Policy," Globe and Mail, Report on Business, 2 Dec. 1982, B3.

Unsigned newspaper article:

> [17]"Financing System Called Damaging to National Growth,"
> Globe and Mail, 14 July 1982, 4.

Footnotes for subsequent references

1. Subsequent footnote references should usually be brief, including only the author's name and the page number:

   Morton, 22.

2. Instead of putting subsequent references as footnotes, you may enclose them in parentheses and include them in the body of the text, before the final punctuation in the referring sentence:

   > Educators can also be trendy; the charge may be fair that those who deplore a return to the basics are "suffering from delirium trendens" (Hornyansky, 93).

3. If you are citing more than one work by an author, add the title (it may be in shortened form) after the author's name:

   (Frye: Modern Century, 42)

4. If you are repeatedly referring to a single primary source, in references after the first you may simply enclose the page numbers in parentheses. If you are discussing a drama, refer to the act, scene, and line; if discussing a poem, refer to the verse and/or line.

BIBLIOGRAPHIES

A bibliography is an alphabetical list of both those works cited in an essay and those found useful in preparing it. Your instructor may not require a bibliography if you document your references fully in footnotes, but it's a good idea to provide one.

Format

The format for bibliographies differs slightly from that for footnotes:
1. Use a separate page at the end of your essay, with an underlined heading, *Bibliography*, centred on the page.
2. Single-space all entries, leaving a double space between entries and a triple space between the heading and the first entry. Do not indent entries.
3. Do not number entries, but *list them alphabetically* by the author's

or editor's surname. If no author is given, begin with the first significant word in the title.
4. Begin each bibliographic entry at the margin and indent any subsequent line five spaces.
5. Separate the main divisions by periods (rather than the commas and parentheses used in footnotes).

Book:

> Fox, Paul W., ed. Politics: Canada. 4th ed. Toronto: McGraw-Hill Ryerson, 1977.

> Frye, Northrop. Anatomy of Criticism: Four Essays. Princeton: Princeton Univ. Press, 1957.

If you include more than one work by a particular author, place the entries in alphabetical order by title (not counting the initial articles). Give the name in the first entry only. For subsequent entries, type ten hyphens and a period. Leave two spaces and give the next title:

> Hood, Hugh. The Governor's Bridge Is Closed. Toronto: Oberon, 1973.

> ----------. A New Athens. Toronto: Oberon, 1977.

If there is more than one author or editor, use inverted order for the first name only and natural order for the rest:

> Thomas, Clara and John Lennox. William Arthur Deacon: A Canadian Literary Life. Toronto: Univ. of Toronto Press, 1982.

Article in a book:

> Ward, Barbara. "The First International Nation." In Canada: A Guide to the Peaceable Kingdom, 45-9. William Kilbourn, ed. Toronto: Macmillan, 1970.

Article in a journal:

> Heath, Jeffrey M. "The Private Language of Evelyn Waugh." English Studies in Canada 2, no. 3 (Fall 1976), 329-39.

NEW MLA SYSTEM FOR THE HUMANITIES

One of the most respected authorities on documentation, the Modern Language Association of America, has recently recommended a new system of documentation for the humanities. This new system is closer to the one used in the sciences and social sciences. Short parenthetical citations in the text correspond to more detailed bibliographical entries at the end of the paper, and the bibliography itself lists only those works cited. This format eliminates footnotes except for those giving explanatory comments.

Be careful when using this system. Since the bibliography includes only those works you mention in the text, you may inadvertently fail to give credit to works you have found helpful in preparing your paper. To avoid the danger of plagiarism, you must make an effort to cite in the text all the works that helped to shape your opinions.

Here is an outline of the new MLA system for the most common types of citation.

In the text

1. Put in parentheses (round brackets) only the information needed to identify a source clearly — usually the author's (or editor's) last name and the page of the text referred to:

   > This type of musical parody is often "conservative in impulse" (Hutcheon 92).

   Place the parentheses where there is a pause in the sentence (usually at the end).

2. If the author's name is already given in the text, put in parentheses only the place of the reference:

   > Harris sees the logic in Hegel's argument (72–74).

Variations

- If you are citing an entire work, try to include the author's (or editor's) name in the text rather than in parentheses:

   > In A Theory of Parody, Linda Hutcheon examines a range of contemporary art forms.

- For literary works, it may sometimes be more appropriate to cite information other than the page number — for example, the chapter, act and scene, or stanza. Unless your instructor prefers otherwise, use arabic numbers for these place numbers. For well-known literary works that you are citing repeatedly, you can use abbreviated titles, such as *MND* for *A Midsummer Night's Dream*:

   > This image of marriage is echoed in the later comedy (MND 4.2).

- If the work has more than one author, give all the names or add
  et al. to the first name (whichever form you use in the bibliography):

  The same argument was applied to the universities
  (Matthews and Steele 50–62).

- If the work is listed by title, give the title or a shortened version
  of it.
- If the work has a corporate author (for example, Government of
  Ontario), give the name of the organization or a shortened form.
- If the citation follows a quotation, place the parentheses after
  any quotation marks but before the end punctuation:

  The result, some claim, is "cultural suicide" (Jones et al.
  42–42).

- If you are citing two or more works by the same author, include
  the appropriate title with each citation.

In the bibliography

1. List only those works you have cited in the text.
2. At the top centre of the page, put the underlined title *Bibliography* or *List of Works Cited*.
3. Use the same format and style as for the bibliography in the
   traditional humanities system (see pp. 121–2).

Footnotes

You do not need footnotes in the new MLA system. They are useful
only if you want to explain something you have said in the text: these
are content notes.

Do not put vital information in a footnote. At the same time, try to
avoid footnotes that are really just information dumps — repositories
for bits of detail you don't know what else to do with.

When you do need footnotes, use the same format as in the traditional humanities system (see Format, pp. 117–18).

CATCHLIST
of misused words
and phrases

accept, except. Accept is a verb meaning to *receive affirmatively*; **except**, when used as a verb, means to *exclude*:

> I <u>accept</u> your offer.
> The teacher <u>excepted</u> him from the general punishment.

accompanied by, accompanied with. Use **accompanied by** for people; **accompanied with** for objects:

> He was <u>accompanied</u> by his wife.
> The brochure arrived, <u>accompanied with</u> a discount coupon.

advice, advise. Advice is a noun, **advise** a verb:

> He was <u>advised</u> to ignore the others' <u>advice</u>.

affect, effect. As a verb to **affect** means to *influence*; as a noun it's a technical psychological term. The verb to **effect** means to *bring about*. The noun means *result*. In most cases, you will be safe if you remember to use **affect** for the verb and **effect** for the noun:

> The eye drops <u>affect</u> his vision.
> The <u>effect</u> of higher government spending is higher inflation.

all together, altogether. All together means *in a group*; **altogether** is an adverb meaning *entirely*:

> He was <u>altogether</u> certain that the children were <u>all together</u>.

alot. Write as two separate words: *a lot*.

allusion, illusion. An **allusion** is an indirect reference to something; an **illusion** is a false perception:

> The rock image is an <u>allusion</u> to the myth of Sisyphus.
> He thought he saw a sea monster, but it was an <u>illusion</u>.

among, between. Use **among** for three or more persons or objects, **between** for two:

> Between you and me, there's trouble among the team members.

amoral, immoral. Amoral means *non-moral* or outside the moral sphere; **immoral** means *wicked*:

> As an art critic, he was amoral in his judgements.
> That immoral performance should be restricted to adults.

amount, number. Use **amount** for money or noncountable quantities; use **number** for countable items:

> No amount of wealth or number of expensive possessions will make up for a lack of love.

anyways. Non-standard English: use *anyway*.

as, because. As is a weaker conjunction than **because** and may be confused with *when*:

> As I was working, I ate at my desk.
> Because I was working, I ate at my desk.

> He arrived as I was leaving.
> He arrived when I was leaving.

as to. A common feature of bureaucratese; replace it with a single-word preposition such as *about* or *on*:

> ✗ They were concerned as to the range of disagreement.
> ✓ They were concerned about the range of disagreement.

> ✗ They recorded his comments as to the treaty.
> ✓ They recorded his comments on the treaty.

bad, badly. Bad is an adjective meaning *not good*:

> The meat tastes bad.
> He felt bad about forgetting the dinner party.

Badly is an adverb meaning *not well;* when used with the verbs **want** or **need**, it means *very much*:

> She thought he played the villain's part badly.
> I badly need a new suit.

beside, besides. Beside is a preposition meaning *next to*:

> She worked beside her assistant.

Besides has two uses: as a preposition it means *in addition to*; as a conjunctive adverb it means *moreover*:

> Besides recommending the changes, the consultants are implementing them.
> Besides, it was hot and we wanted to rest.

between. See **among**.

bring, take. One **brings** something to a closer place and **takes** it to a farther one.

can, may. Can means to *be able*; **may** means to *have permission*:

> Can you fix the lock?
> May I have another piece of cake?

In speech, **can** is used to cover both meanings: in formal writing, however, you should observe the distinction.

can't hardly. A faulty combination of the phrases **can't** and **can hardly**. Use one or the other of them instead:

> He can't swim.
> He can hardly swim.

capital, capitol. As a noun **capital** may refer to a seat of government, the top of a pillar, an upper-case letter, or accumulated wealth. **Capitol** refers only to a specific American—or ancient Roman—legislative building.

complement, compliment. The verb to **complement** means to *complete*; to **compliment** means to *praise*:

> His engineering skill complements the skills of the designers.
> I complimented her on her outstanding report.

continual, continuous. Continual means *repeated over a period of time*; **continuous** means *constant* or *without interruption*:

> The strikes caused continual delays in building the road.
> In August, it rained continuously for five days.

could of. Incorrect, as are **might of, should of,** and **would of.** Replace **of** with *have*:

   ✗ He <u>could of</u> done it.
   ✓ He <u>could have</u> done it.
   ✓ They <u>might have</u> been there.
   ✓ I <u>should have</u> known.
   ✓ We <u>would have</u> left earlier.

council, counsel. Council is a noun meaning an *advisory* or *deliberative assembly*. **Counsel** as a noun means *advice* or *lawyer*; as a verb it means to *give advice*:

> The college <u>council</u> meets on Tuesday.
> We respect his <u>counsel</u>, since he's seldom wrong.
> As a camp <u>counsellor</u>, you may need to <u>counsel</u> parents as well as children.

criterion, criteria. A **criterion** is a standard for judging something. **Criteria** is the plural of **criterion** and thus requires a plural verb:

> <u>These</u> are my <u>criteria</u> for selecting the paintings.

data. The plural of *datum*, **data** is increasingly treated as a singular noun, but this usage is not yet acceptable in formal prose: use a plural verb.

different than. Incorrect. Use either **different from** (American usage) or **different to** (British).

disinterested, uninterested. Disinterested implies impartiality or neutrality; **uninterested** implies a lack of interest:

> As a <u>disinterested</u> observer, he was in a good position to judge the issue fairly.
> <u>Uninterested</u> in the proceedings, he yawned repeatedly.

due to. Although increasingly used to mean *because of*, **due** is an adjective and therefore needs to modify something:

   ✗ <u>Due to</u> his impatience, we lost the contract. [<u>Due</u> is dangling]
   ✓ The loss was <u>due to</u> his impatience.

farther, further. Farther refers to distance, **further** to extent:

> He paddled <u>farther</u> than his friends.
> He explained the plan <u>further</u>.

good, well. Good is an adjective, not an adverb. **Well** can be both: as an adverb, it means *effectively*; as an adjective, it means *healthy*:

The pear sauce tastes good.
She is a good golfer.
She plays golf well.
At last, he is well again after his long bout of flu.

hanged, hung. Hanged means *executed by hanging*. **Hung** means *suspended* or *clung to*:

He was hanged at dawn for the murder.
He hung the picture.
He hung to the boat when it capsized.

hopefully. Use **hopefully** as an adverb meaning *full of hope*:

She scanned the horizon hopefully, waiting for her friend's ship to appear.

In formal writing, using **hopefully** to mean *I hope* is still frowned upon, although increasingly common; it's better to use *I hope*:

✗ Hopefully we'll make a bigger profit this year.
✓ I hope we'll make a bigger profit this year.

imply, infer. Imply refers to what a statement suggests; **infer** relates to the audience's interpretation:

His letter implied that he was lonely.
I inferred from his letter that he would welcome a visit.

irregardless. Redundant; use *regardless*.

its, it's. Its is a form of possessive pronoun; **it's** is a contraction of *it is*. Many people mistakenly put an apostrophe in **its** in order to show possession:

✗ The cub wanted it's mother.
✓ The cub wanted its mother.
✓ It's time to leave.

less, fewer. Use **less** for money and things that are not countable; use **fewer** for things that are:

Now that he's earning less money he's going to fewer movies.

lie, lay. To **lie** means to *assume a horizontal position*; to **lay** means to *put down*. The changes of tense often cause confusion:

Present	Past	Past participle
lie	lay	lain
lay	laid	laid

like, as. **Like** is a preposition, but it is often wrongly used as a conjunction. To join two independent clauses, use the conjunction **as**:

   ✗ I want to progress <u>like</u> you have this year.
   ✓ I want to progress <u>as</u> you have this year.

   ✓ Prof. Dodd is <u>like</u> my old school principal.

might of. See **could of.**

myself, me. **Myself** is an intensifier of, not a substitute for, *I* or *me*:

   ✗ He gave it to John and <u>myself</u>.
   ✓ He gave it to John and <u>me</u>.

   ✗ Jane and <u>myself</u> are invited.
   ✓ Jane and <u>I</u> are invited.

   ✓ <u>Myself</u>, I would prefer a swivel chair.

nor, or. Use **nor** with **neither** and **or** by itself or with **either**:

    He is <u>neither</u> overworked <u>nor</u> underfed.
    The plant is <u>either</u> diseased <u>or</u> dried out.

off of. Remove the unnecessary **of**:

   ✗ The fence kept the children <u>off of</u> the premises.
   ✓ The fence kept the children <u>off</u> the premises.

phenomenon. A singular noun: the plural is **phenomena.**

principal, principle. As an adjective, **principal** means *main* or *most important*; a **principal** is the *head of a school.* A **principle** is a *law* or *controlling idea:*

    Our <u>principal</u> aim is to reduce the deficit.
    Our <u>principal</u>, Prof. Smart, retires next year.
    We are defending the island as a matter of <u>principle</u>.

rational, rationale. **Rational** is an adjective meaning *logical* or *able to reason.* **Rationale** is a noun meaning *explanation*:

    That was not a <u>rational</u> decision.
    The president sent around a memo with a <u>rationale</u> for his proposal.

real, really. The adjective **real** should never be used as an adverb; use *really* instead:

   ✓ We had <u>real</u> maple syrup with our pancakes.

   ✗ It was <u>real</u> good.
   ✓ It was <u>really</u> good.

set, sit. To **sit** means to *rest on the buttocks*; to **set** means to *put* or *place*:

> After standing so long, you'll want to sit down.
> Please set the bowl on the table.

should of. See **could of.**

their, there. **Their** is the possessive form of the third person plural pronoun. **There** is usually an adverb, meaning *at that place* or *at that point*; sometimes it is used as an expletive (an introductory word in a sentence):

> They parked their bikes there.
> There is no point in arguing with you.

to, too, two. **To** is a preposition, as well as part of the infinitive form of a verb:

> We went to town in order to shop.

Too is an adjective showing degree (the soup is *too* hot) or an adverb meaning *moreover*. **Two** is the spelled version of the number 2.

while. To avoid misreadings, use **while** only when you mean *at the same time that*. Do not use it as a substitute for *although*, *whereas*, or *but*:

> ✗ While he's getting fair marks, he'd like to do better.
> ✗ I headed for home, while she decided to stay.
> ✓ He fell asleep while he was reading.

-wise. Never use **-wise** as a suffix to form new words when you mean *with regard to*:

> ✗ Sales-wise, the company did better last year.
> (or) The company's sales increased last year.

would have, would of. When people are describing a hypothetical instance in the past, they often mistakenly use **would have** in both the condition (*if*) clause and the consequence clause: see p. 79. For **would of,** see *could of.*

your, you're. **Your** is a pronominal adjective used to show possession; **you're** is a contraction of *you are*:

> You're likely to miss your train.

GLOSSARY

abstract
a summary accompanying a formal scientific report or paper, briefly outlining the contents.

abstract language
theoretical language removed from concrete particulars: e.g., *justice, goodness, truth* (cf. **concrete language**).

acronym
a word made up of the first letters of a group of words: e.g., *NATO* for *North Atlantic Treaty Organization*.

active voice
see **voice**.

adjective
a word that modifies or describes a noun or pronoun, hence a kind of noun marker: e.g., *red, beautiful, solemn.* An **adjectival phrase** or **adjectival clause** is a group of words modifying a noun or pronoun.

adverb
a word that modifies or qualifies a verb, adjective, or adverb, often answering a question such as *how? why? when?* or *where?*: e.g., *slowly, fortunately, early, abroad.* An **adverbial phrase** or **adverbial clause** is a group of words modifying a verb, adjective, or adverb: e.g., *by force, in revenge.* See also **conjunctive adverb**.

agreement
consistency in tense, number, or person between related parts of a sentence: e.g., between subject and verb, or noun and related pronoun.

ambiguity
vague or equivocal language; meaning that can be taken two ways.

antecedent (referent)
the noun for which a pronoun stands.

appositive
a word or phrase that identifies a preceding noun or pronoun: e.g., *Mrs. Jones,* **my aunt,** *is sick.* The second phrase is said to be *in apposition* to the first.

article
a word that precedes a noun and shows whether the noun is definite or indefinite; a kind of determiner or noun-marker. **Indefinite article:** *a (an).* **Definite article**: *the.*

assertion
a positive statement or claim: e.g., *The Senate is irrelevant.*

auxiliary
a verb used in combination with another verb to create a verb phrase; a helping verb used to create certain tenses and emphases: e.g., *could, do, may, will, have.*

bibliography

(a) a list of works referred to or found useful in the preparation of an essay or report; (b) a reference book listing works available in a particular subject.

case

the inflected form of pronouns (see **inflection**). **Subjective case**: *I, we, he, she, it, they.* **Objective case**: *me, us, him, her, it, them.* **Possessive case**: *my , our, his, her, its, their.*

circumlocution

a roundabout or circuitous expression: e.g., *in a family way* for *pregnant*; *at this point in time* for *now*.

clause

a group of words containing a subject and predicate. An **independent clause** can stand by itself as a complete sentence: e.g., *I bought a hamburger.* A **subordinate** or **dependent clause** cannot stand by itself but must be connected to another clause: e.g., **Since I was hungry,** *I bought a hamburger.*

cliché

a trite or well-worn expression that has lost its impact through overuse: e.g., *slept like a log, sunny disposition, tried and true.*

collective noun

a noun that is singular in form but refers to a group: e.g., *family, team, jury.* It may take either a singular or a plural verb, depending on whether it refers to individual members or to the group as a whole.

comma splice

see **run-on sentence**.

complement

a completing word or phrase that usually follows a linking verb to form a **subjective complement**: e.g., (1) *He is* **my father.** (2) *That cigar smells* **terrible.** If the complement is an adjective it is sometimes called a **predicate adjective.** An **objective complement** completes the direct object rather than the subject: e.g., *We found him* **honest and trustworthy.**

complex sentence

a sentence containing a dependent clause as well as an independent one: e.g., *I bought the ring, although it was expensive.*

compound sentence

a sentence containing two or more independent clauses: e.g., *I saw the car wreck and I reported it.* A sentence is called **compound-complex** if it contains a dependent clause as well as two independent ones: e.g., *When the fog lifted, I saw the car wreck and I reported it.*

conclusion

the part of an essay in which the findings are pulled together or implications revealed so that the reader has a sense of closure or completion. In a business report the conclusion is sometimes placed at the front.

concrete language

specific language, giving particular details (often details of sense): e.g., *red, corduroy dress, three long-stemmed roses* (cf. **abstract language**).

conjunction
an uninflected word used to
link words, phrases, or clauses.
A **coordinating conjunction**
(e.g., *and, or, but, for, yet*) links
two equal parts of a sentence.
A **subordinating conjunction**,
placed at the beginning of a
subordinate clause, shows the
logical dependence of that clause
on another: e.g., (1) **Although**
I am poor, I am happy. (2) **While**
others slept, he studied. **Correlative
conjunctions** are pairs of
coordinating conjunctions (see
correlatives).

conjunctive adverb
a type of adverb that shows the
logical relation between the
phrase or clause that it modifies
and a preceding one: e.g.,
(1) *I sent the letter; it never arrived,*
however. (2) *The battery died;*
therefore *the car wouldn't start.*

connotation
associative meaning; the range of
suggestion called up by a certain
word. Apparent synonyms, such
as *poor* and *underprivileged*, may
have different connotations (cf.
denotation).

context
the text surrounding a particular
passage that helps to establish its
meaning.

contraction
a word formed by combining and
shortening two words: e.g., *isn't,
can't, we're.*

coordinate construction
see **correlatives**.

coordinating conjunction
see **conjunction**

copula verb
see **linking verb**.

correlatives (coordinates)
pairs of coordinating conjunctions:
e.g., *either/or, neither/nor, not only/but.*

dangling modifier
a modifying word or phrase
(often a participial phrase) that is
not grammatically connected to
any part of the sentence: e.g.,
Walking to school, *the street was
slippery.*

demonstrative pronoun
a pronoun that points out
something: e.g., (1) **This** *is his
reason.* (2) **That** *looks like my lost
earring.* When used to modify a
noun or pronoun, a demonstrative
pronoun becomes a kind of
pronominal adjective: e.g., *this
hat, those people.*

denotation
the literal or dictionary meaning
of a word (cf. **connotation**).

diction
the choice of words with regard to
their tone, degree of formality,
or register. Formal diction is the
language of orations and serious
essays. The informal diction of
everyday speech or conversational
writing can, at its extreme,
become slang.

discourse
talk, either oral or written.
Direct discourse gives the actual
words spoken or written: e.g.,
Donne said, **"No man is an
island."** In writing, direct discourse is put in quotation marks.

Indirect discourse gives the meaning of the speech rather than the actual words. In writing, indirect discourse is not put in quotation marks: e.g., *He said that no one exists in an island of isolation.*

ellipsis marks
three spaced periods indicating an omission from a quoted passage.

endnote
a footnote or citation placed at the end of an essay or report.

essay
a literary composition on any subject. Some essays are descriptive or narrative, but in an academic setting most are expository (explanatory) or argumentative.

expletive
a grammatically meaningless exclamation or phrase. The most common expletives are the sentence beginnings *It is* and *There is (are)*.

exploratory writing
the informal writing done to help generate ideas before formal planning begins.

footnote
a citation placed at the bottom of a page or the end of the composition (cf. **endnote**).

fused sentence
see **run-on sentence**.

general language
language lacking specific details; abstract language.

gerund
a verbal (part-verb) that functions as a noun and is marked by an -*ing* ending: e.g., **Swimming** *can help you become fit.*

grammar
a study of the forms and relations of words, and of the rules governing their use in speech and writing.

hypothesis
a supposition or trial proposition made as a starting point for further investigation.

hypothetical instance
a supposed occurrence; often shown by a clause beginning with *if.*

Indefinite article
a (an). Definite article: *the.*

independent clause
see **clause**.

indirect discourse
see **discourse**.

infinitive
a type of verbal not connected to any subject: e.g., *to ask.* The **base infinitive** omits the *to*: e.g., *ask.*

inflection
the change in the form of a word to indicate number, person, case, tense, or degree.

integrate
combine or blend together.

intensifier (qualifier)
a word that modifies and adds emphasis to another word or phrase: e.g., **very** *tired*, **quite** *happy*, *I* **myself**.

interjection
a remark or exlamation interposed or thrown into a speech, usually accompanied by an exclamation mark: e.g., *Oh dear! Alas!*

interrogative sentence
a sentence that asks a question: e.g., *What is the time?*

intransitive verb
a verb that does not take a direct object: e.g., *fall, sleep, talk.*

italics
slanting type used for emphasis, replaced in typescript by underlining.

jargon
technical terms used unnecessarily or in inappropriate places: e.g., *peer-group interaction* for *friendship.*

linking verb (copula verb)
the verb *to be* used to join subject to complement: e.g., *The apples* were *ripe.*

literal meaning
the primary, or denotative, meaning of a word.

logical indicator
a word or phrase—usually a conjunction or conjunctive adverb— that shows the logical relation between sentences or clauses: e.g., *since, furthermore, therefore.*

modifier
a word or group of words that describes or limits another element in the sentence. A **misplaced modifier** causes confusion because it is not placed next to the element it should modify: e.g., *I only ate the pie.* [Revised: *I ate only the pie.*]

mood
(a) as a grammatical term, the form that shows a verb's function (indicative, imperative, interrogative, or subjunctive);
(b) when applied to literature generally, the state of mind or feeling shown.

non-restrictive element
see **restrictive element**

noun
an inflected part of speech marking a person, place, thing, idea, action, or feeling, and usually serving as subject, object, or complement. A **common noun** is a general term: e.g., *dog, paper, automobile.* A **proper noun** is a specific name: e.g., *Mary, Sudburv. Skidoo.*

object
(a) a noun or pronoun that, when it completes the action of a verb, is called a **direct object**: e.g., *He passed the* **puck**. An **indirect object** is the person or thing receiving the direct object: e.g., *He passed the* **puck** (direct object) *to* **Richard** (indirect object).
(b) The noun or pronoun in a group of words beginning with a preposition; pronouns take the objective case: e.g., *at the* house, *about* **her**, *for* **me**.

objective complement
see **complement**.

objectivity
a disinterested stance; a position taken without personal bias or prejudice (cf. **subjectivity**).

outline
with regard to an essay or report, a brief sketch of the main parts; a written plan.

paragraph
a unit of sentences arranged logically to explain or describe an idea, event, or object; usually marked by indentation of the first line.

parallel wording
wording in which a series of items has a similar grammatical form: e.g., *At her marriage my grandmother promised* **to love, to honour, and to obey** *her husband.*

paraphrase
restate in different words.

parentheses
curved lines, enclosing and setting off a passage; not to be confused with square brackets.

parenthetical element
an interrupting word or phrase: e.g., *My musical career,* **if it can be called that,** *consisted of playing the triangle in kindergarten.*

participle
a verbal (part-verb) that functions as an adjective. Participles can be either **present**, usually marked by an *-ing* ending (e.g., *taking*), or **past** (*having taken*); they can also be passive (*having been taken*).

parts of speech
the major classes of words. Some grammarians include only function words (nouns, verbs, adjectives, and adverbs); others also include pronouns, prepositions, conjunctions, and interjections.

passive voice
see **voice**.

past participle
see **participle**.

periodic sentence
a sentence in which the normal order is inverted or an essential element suspended until the very end: e.g., *Out of the house, past the grocery store, through the school yard and down the railroad tracks* **raced the frightened boy**.

person
in grammar, the three classes of personal pronouns referring to the person speaking (first person), person spoken to (second person), and person spoken about (third person). With verbs, only the third person singular has a distinctive form.

personal pronoun
see **pronoun**.

phrase
a unit of words lacking a subject-predicate combination. The most common kind is the **prepositional phrase**—a unit comprising preposition plus object. Some modern grammarians also refer to the **single-word phrase**.

plural
indicating two or more in number. Nouns, pronouns, and verbs all have plural forms.

possessive case
see **case**.

prefix
a syllable placed in front of the root form of a word to make a new word: e.g., *pro-, in-, sub-* (cf. **suffix**).

preposition
a short word heading a unit of words containing an object, thus forming a **prepositional phrase:** e.g., **under** *the tree,* **before** *my time.*

pronoun
a word that stands in for a noun. **A personal pronoun** stands in for the name of a person: *I*, *he*, *she*, *we*, *they*, etc.
p. 120

punctuation
a conventional system of signs used to indicate stops or divisions in a sentence and to make meaning clearer: e.g., comma, period, semicolon, etc.

reference works
material consulted when preparing an essay or report.

referent (antecedent)
the noun for which a pronoun stands.

register
the degree of formality in word choice and sentence structure.

relative clause
a clause headed by a relative pronoun: e.g., *the man* **who came to dinner** *is my uncle*.

relative pronoun
who, *which*, *what*, *that*, or their compounds beginning an adjective or noun clause: e.g., *the house* **that** *Jack built*; **whatever** *you say*.

restrictive element
a phrase or clause that identifies or is essential to the meaning of a term: e.g., *The book* **that I need** *is lost*. It should not be set off by commas. A non-restrictive element is not needed to identify the term and is usually set off by commas: e.g., *This book*, **which I got from my aunt**, *is one of my favourites*.

run-on sentence
a sentence that goes on beyond the point where it should have stopped. The term covers both the **comma splice** (two sentences joined by a comma) and the **fused sentence** (two sentences joined without any punctuation between them).

sentence
a grammatical unit that includes both a subject and a predicate. The end of a sentence is marked by a period.

sentence fragment
a group of words lacking either a subject or a verb; an incomplete sentence.

simple sentence
a sentence made up of only one clause: e.g., *Joan climbed the tree*.

slang
colloquial speech, not considered part of standard English; often used in a special sense by a particular group: e.g., *gross* for *disgusting*; *gig* as a musician's term.

split infinitive
a construction in which a word is placed between *to* and the base verb: e.g., *to completely finish*.

squinting modifier
a kind of misplaced modifier; one that could be connected to elements on either side, making meaning ambiguous: e.g., *When he wrote the letter* **finally** *his boss thanked him*.

standard English
the English currently spoken or written by literate people over a wide geographical area.

subject
in grammar, the noun or noun equivalent about which something is predicated; that part of a clause with which the verb agrees: e.g., **They** *swim every day when the* **pool** *is open.*

subjective complement
see **complement**

subjectivity
a personal stance, not impartial (cf. **objectivity**).

subordinate clause
see **clause**.

subordinating conjunction
see **conjunction**.

subordination
making one clause in a sentence dependent on another.

suffix
an addition placed at the end of a word to form a derivative: e.g., *prepare—prepara***tion**; *sing—sing***ing** (cf. **prefix**).

synonym
a word with the same dictionary meaning as another word: e.g., *begin* and *commence*.

syntax
sentence construction; the grammatical relations of words.

tense
the time reference of verbs.

theme
a recurring or dominant idea.

thesis statement
a one-sentence assertion that gives the central argument of an essay or thesis.

topic sentence
the sentence in a paragraph that expresses the main or controlling idea.

transition word
a word that shows the logical relation between sentences or parts of a sentence and thus helps to signal the change from one idea to another: e.g., *therefore, also, accordingly.*

transitive verb
one that takes an object: e.g., *hit, bring, cover.*

usage
accepted practice.

verb
that part of a predicate expressing an action, state of being, or condition, telling what a subject is or does. Verbs inflect to show tense (time). The principal parts of a verb are the three basic forms from which all tenses are made: the base infinitive, the past tense, and the past participle.

verbal
a word that is similar in form to a verb but does not function as one: a participle, a gerund, or an infinitive.

voice
the form of a verb that shows whether the subject acted (active voice) or was acted upon (passive voice): e.g., *He* **hit** *the ball* (active). *The ball* **was hit** *by him* (passive). Only transitive verbs (verbs taking objects) can be passive.

Index

NOTE: Grammatical terms not listed here are explained in the glossary.